To Melani,

May God Bless
You Always –
Robert B
Psalm 37.5

The Visitor

Three Wishes for a Life

Merry Christmas !
2016 !

By
Robert Bush

xulon
PRESS

Dedicated to:

To my wife and daughters:

Thank you for your constant support, as you've provided me with the encouragement I've needed in order to passionately pursue my dream. Our books are helping numerous people on a daily basis, but none of this would have been possible had it not been for your unconditional love. I have learned so much from the three of you, but more than anything, you've provided me with a daily reminder of just how truly blessed I am. Your eyes continually sparkle with a passion for God that can never be replaced or taken away...and for that, I am grateful.

To my parents:

You have done so many things for me...I have no idea where to begin. In order for me to somehow capture the impact you've had on my life, I need to peel back all of the layers and go directly to the core. Without a doubt, the greatest gift you've given me is the realization that you have loved me regardless of the circumstance. Having this peace of mind has allowed me to be a better father as well because I know how important it is for our children. Thank you for showing me the true definition of love. In my heart, I have always known that you love me…and I know this can never be taken away.

To all the orphans who wake up each and every day without a mother or father:

As a child, can you imagine crying yourself to sleep at night, knowing that you were all alone? It's hard to imagine anything more painful than growing up without the love of a parent, but this is the case for thousands of children each and every day. I hope and pray that this book provides an impetus for the reader to step out in faith and touch the life of a child in some way. The transformation of Benjamin Sanders clearly reflects the impact we can all have if love is the focal point of what we do…how each of us truly can make a difference.

To each and every one of us who struggles with the numerous challenges (spiritual, emotional, and financial) that life brings:

The dichotomy of doing what we have to do versus doing what we want to do is one of the greatest obstacles we all face. No matter how hard we try to avoid the temptations that surround us, the world constantly pulls us in a different direction than many of us want to go. It is unrealistic to think that the financial turmoil we all face in our world today is not going to create personal challenges regarding our own spiritual walk. However, our ability to focus on what we need rather than what we want is one of the most important first steps we can take in our own personal journey. *The Visitor...Three Wishes for a Life* is designed to provide the initiative for every reader to honestly look within their own soul regarding what truly is important in life. Our ability to identify our priorities, with faith and family at the top of the list, is a necessary first step. If we place our trust in man, we will be disappointed. Our goal should be to always keep our eyes focused on Him, as reflected in 2 Timothy 4:7, which reads, *"I have fought the good fight, I have finished the race, I have kept the faith."* Regardless of the world we live in, and the constant pressures around us, this needs to be our ultimate goal. We must never take our eyes off the real prize.

Table of Contents

Chapter One

The Playing Field

T he man leaned back in his cell and felt his eyes begin to close because it had been almost 48 hours since he had gotten any rest at all. His only hope right now was to somehow find a way to go back in time and erase the events that would forever change the lives of many. His entire life had been turned upside down, and the chances of him ever getting it back again would be impossible. Too many lives had been ruined because of his selfish act, even though his actions weren't intentional. As he stared at the ceiling, he began to hear the sounds of clicking in the distance. At first, the noise sounded like the tapping of a hollowed out object in one of the cells at the other end of the unit he now called home. However, as the noise began to gain momentum and moved closer to his bed, it became apparent to him that it was a set of heeled shoes that somehow made their way into the complex with his neighboring inmates. The man could tell the noise was slowly moving his way, and his hope was for it to either stop or veer off in another direction…but this wasn't the case. The clicking noise continued to get closer and closer, until it finally stopped just outside his cell door. The man rubbed his eyes and looked up toward the dark figure that was standing outside his new 8' x 10' home. He continued to rub his eyes even harder than before, hoping the figure would disappear, but it continued to stare his way. The man peered into the face of the person who was now just inches from the bars that separated them, but there were no discernible features…only the shadow from the scarf that seemed to be draped across the top of the figure's head. The man looked up and said, "Do I know you? What do you want with me?" The dark figure reached out and slowly began to slide her gloved hand through the bars in the cell. "My name is Celeste, and I have been assigned to you. What I am about to tell you will have a dramatic impact on your life. It will be unlike anything you've ever been part of before, and depending on the course of action you take, your life will be changed forever. You need to listen to me very carefully because you will not have a lot of time to make the most important decision of your life. Over the course of the next year, I will be paying three visits to you, tonight is the first of those three. I am here, quite frankly, because your life has spun out of control…and this is just the beginning. I know all about the events over the past two days, but I am here to provide you with an option that may alleviate the painful path you are heading down. Tonight, I am going to show you the playing field that will ultimately determine your out-come. As you and I both know, the accident that took place two nights ago was caused by your personal negligence, and unpredictable temper, that surfaced due to the phone call that interrupted your quiet drive home. This may or may not come out in the upcoming trial that will soon consume you, but I know what you were doing when your car veered off the side of the highway. I know the frame of mind you were in when your car spun out of control. My next two visits will be impacted by the way you proceed from here and how you handle the details of the events that have transpired. I will be granting you three wishes that will undoubtedly impact your life. The first wish, should you decide to choose it, will be granted before I leave here tonight. Your second wish will coincide with my second visit, which will take place exactly six months from today. Your third and final wish will be granted one year from today...and then I will go away. I must caution you that my job over the course of this next year is not to influence your decision or tell you what to do. My only real purpose here is to show you a glimpse of the future, but I will not be providing you with any direction regarding the path you decide to follow. I must caution you. Your chosen path will not only impact your outcome here in this world, but it will also determine your ultimate fate as well. Do not ask me what this means because, in due time, you will find out for yourself. Now, let's go back to the event that has brought us together here tonight. You may want to close your eyes and take a deep breath. This is not going to be easy for you, but do not despise me for being the messenger here tonight. Remember...my job is to not allow any personal emotion on my part to enter into the equation.

There will be emotion, but that will more than likely only come from you. My purpose is not to express anything other than total objectivity when it comes to your life's path and eventual outcome. That ultimate decision will be made by you. However, once you have made your three wishes, then you will be forced to live with the outcome of your choices. There will be no turning back, and you will be playing out your life based on the decisions you've made. Therefore, it will be very important for you to really think through your wishes because once they are set in motion, there is no turning back. There is one very important thing you need to fully understand. We cannot change the events of the past; however, we can directly influence them based upon the implementation of your requested wish. In essence, if you ask me to grant a wish, then you need to believe that this specific wish will better prepare you to overcome the events of your past. So…you need to make sure that if you decide to move forward, the wish you choose must be thought through very carefully. Now, let's go back to the event that brought us to this point here tonight…the reason as to why I am here. The evening in question started out like so many others, both for you and for them. But, as you well know, that would soon change. Now, close your eyes so we can go back in time, to the night that could forever haunt you…depending on how you decide to proceed from here." Edward looked over at the dark face that seemed to mesmerize him and almost hypnotize his every thought. He slowly closed his eyes and began to replay the events that felt like they happened just minutes ago.

The drive home never took more than 45 minutes because Edward always tried to capitalize on this quiet time. He always did his best to think through specific issues that had evolved over the course of the day. Today would turn out to be different than all the rest, as his mind was working overtime with thoughts that he just couldn't shake free. His company had been confronted with their greatest challenge to date, and his law firm was beginning to feel the crunch of the economic times around them. Work had been the sole focus in Edward's life and had grown into an obsession that had no room for family. Quite frankly, Edward preferred it that way. He had never been married before, as he just never seemed to have the time for anyone else in his highly structured, compartmentalized life. His love of money, and the lifestyle that came with it, had become his sole focus in life since he finished college years ago. Edward's law firm was his family...and his necessity to win at all costs had developed into a game that was defined by only one parameter... the size of his checkbook. Edward had been conditioned long ago to believe that there could never be enough, and that the next deal had to be bigger than the last. However, Edward had found himself in a position now that was similar to many of his colleagues. No matter how hard he tried, Edward was tied to one very important client who continued to fund the majority of his overall revenue attainment...a dangerous position to say the least!

Edward's most important client, Andrew Ridgeley III, had recently gone through a series of ill-advised stock transactions, which caused significant collateral damage for all who knew him. As the economy began to crumble around him, Ridgeley continued to throw good money after bad. He desperately searched for the one big win that would somehow pull him out of his personal hole, but even he was beginning to realize that the probability of this happening now was becoming highly unlikely. Ridgeley continued to push as hard as he could, but the big win never came, and everything he owned was quickly leveraged to the max. Ridgeley's overall influence on Edward's law firm was huge, and his rapid spiral downward quickly began to take Edward's firm with it as well. Ridgeley's problem wasn't his overall portfolio, as he owned numerous properties in the area. His overall asset attainment was significant; however, his short-term liquidity was what Edward needed...and this was where his problem was felt the most. Lack of overall account diversification was always a concern, but as long as Ridgeley was on top, Edward's firm was the primary recipient of the constant revenue stream that was flowing his way. This position of strength was now being tested like never before, and Edward found himself on the receiving end of Ridgeley's bad fortune. On this particular day, everything would quickly come to a head, and all who were associated with Ridgeley would soon feel the impact of his personal collapse. His financial decimation turned out to be far more than Ridgeley could handle, and the news of his untimely demise would travel quickly. Earlier that morning, he was found dead at the wheel of his new sports car. Rumor spread throughout the area that Ridgeley had intentionally veered his car off the side of the road. The end result of the impact was permanent, and everything would immediately change in a matter of seconds. Ridgeley's collision with the tree was direct, as its shattered branches seemed to almost laugh in the face of the mangled mess that once was Ridgeley's pride and joy. He died instantly, and now his problems would simply be passed on to others around him...which would include Edward Conners.

Edward was notified of the accident at 10:00 a.m. that morning and quickly began to assess what this turn of events would mean to his law practice...and to his financial position in the community as well. When he got the word, sadness paid a quick visit to Edward, but it soon gave way to the monetary concern that was his top priority. Ridgeley had always been good for a couple hundred thousand dollars a month, which allowed Edward to maintain the lifestyle that had consumed him many years ago. Edward's representation of Ridgeley had always been a given because Ridgeley's personal life was full of costly habits. As a result, Edward had become the fortunate recipient of his escapades for over a decade. Whether it was representing him in his battle against his competition or properly positioning his beverage company for major tax advantages, Edward could pretty much count on a steady dose of revenue each and every month. All of this would now change with his death, as Ridgeley's wife,

Sylvia, would soon be exerting her newfound authority over Edward's finances. For years, she had referred to him as the piranha, insinuating that his only purpose in life was hanging around for Ridgeley's sizeable payouts that routinely came his way. Sylvia vowed to someday remove Edward from his position as Ridgeley's counselor, and now it looked like she would finally have the opportunity to make this happen. As soon as the word made its way to Edward regarding Ridgeley's death, he found himself scrambling to protect his assets. He needed to get things in place before Sylvia got her teeth into the situation. Edward knew he had to quickly find a way to block her move because she would soon be coming his way. Even though Ridgeley's personal fortune had taken a hit recently, Edward was certain that Ridgeley's balance sheet was far stronger than anyone else realized. Sylvia would more than likely be portraying herself as the victim once again, Edward thought, as he prepared himself for the events that would transpire. He absolutely despised the woman...and the feeling on her part toward him was mutual as well.

As Edward slowly made his way out to the car at the end of the day, his mind felt like it was racing 100 miles an hour. What started out as a normal day in his life had begun to unravel with no warning signs whatsoever, and now he was left with nothing but the fear of losing everything. Edward quickly made his way out to the main thoroughfare, which meant that he was now less than 30 minutes from home. He slowly began to rub the back of his neck, hoping that the tension would somehow find another place to reside. Almost simultaneously, he also ran his hand through his uncombed hair, trying desperately to find a way to alleviate the pressure that had made its way to the front of his head as well. Just as Edward was starting to feel a slight sense of reprieve from the events of the day, his cell phone rang with a deafening sound that seemed to be calling out his name. This untimely ring would set the wheels in motion, as Edward's life was about to take an immediate turn for the worse. Waiting on the other end of the line was his nemesis, Sylvia, and she was ready to lay down the gauntlet that had been weighing on her for years. She had been waiting for this opportunity since the day Edward was first introduced to her, and deep down inside, she eagerly anticipated the thought of what was about to unfold. Despite the fact that her husband had been dead for less than 12 hours, this was the call she had dreamed about…and she couldn't wait to show Edward who the real boss was now.

"Hello, this is Edward Conners," Edward answered, as he waited to hear who was waiting for him on the other end of the line. "Edward, this is Sylvia. I'm sure you've already heard about the tragedy that occurred earlier today. We're all still trying to get over our terrible loss, and needless to say, it's been a very rough day. My dear Andrew was loved by many, and his sudden departure is going to have a profound impact on everyone who knew him. However, I'm quickly realizing that I have a number of challenges in front of me, which is the true purpose of my call to you here this evening.

I find myself saddled with not only a terrible loss personally, but Andrew's financial situation was a mess as well. I've already come to the conclusion that I need to move forward on a number of priorities very quickly and try to cut unnecessary expenses as soon as possible. At the top of my cuts, Edward, is you. Quite frankly, you've been sponging off my husband for years, and I'm here to inform you that your little party is over. From this point forward, you'll never see another cent from this family. I've been looking forward to this call for a long time now, ever since the first day I met you. I only wish the circumstances were different, and I still had my Andrew right here by my side to help me deliver this message. Unfortunately, it looks like I'm going to have to do this alone. Edward...even though this is a very sad day for me personally, I'm grateful for the position I am in now because it allows me to do the things I've wanted to do for a very long time. You're on my immediate list of priorities; therefore, it gives me great pleasure to deliver the news that should have come your way a long time ago. Edward... you're fired, effective immediately! My only regret tonight is that I can't be there next to you to see that stupid look on your face right now. This should come as no surprise to you. Good-bye, Edward." Edward could feel the perspiration build on his forehead and slowly drip on to the steering wheel in front of him, while he tried to somehow gather his composure. The woman he despised the most was now in control of the situation, and he didn't like it one bit. In a matter of just one day, his life had been turned upside down, and he knew his business would quickly feel the impact of Sylvia's phone call. Edward's mind began to race, as he mentally assessed his rolodex of clients. Nobody would ever replace his personal loss due to Andrew Ridgeley's death... there just wasn't any way this was possible.

Edward could feel his car begin to pick up speed, but on this particular night, his mind was focused elsewhere. All he could think about was the dollar loss he would soon experience, and the despicable smirk on Sylvia's face that would more than likely never go away. He began to think about all the wonderful places he had visited over the years due to his inflated bank account. His dependency on Andrew had grown from one of monetary security to an expected way of life. Edward could feel his blood begin to boil, while the reality of Andrew's death was slapping him in the face at every turn. His speedometer seemed to be daring him to push harder on the pedal, while the numbers began to climb. Leaning into the turns, Edward could feel his body shift from one side to the other. He was now moving at speeds far greater than the turns in front of him could handle...and Edward could sense that he was beginning to lose control. Sanity paid a much-needed visit to Edward and he quickly brought his speed back down below the required limit, while he regrouped and contemplated his next move. As he began to gather his senses, his phone rang once again, thus delaying his ability to regain the composure that had disappeared over the course of the day. The phone call would not help his situation at all...Sylvia was back for more. "Hello, this is Edward," he said, as he frantically grabbed hold of the phone. Had he known it was Sylvia coming back to torment him even further, he would have just let it continue to ring. "Edward, I'm so sorry to bother you. This is Sylvia again. I forgot to mention to you one other thing a few minutes ago. I need you to return your car in the morning as well. You see, I know all about Andrew's decision to provide you with that beautiful vehicle you've grown to treasure. Since you are no longer working for us, your car is also part of the deal that is being terminated. Thank you, Edward...I do hope you have a nice evening."

Screaming at the top of his lungs, Edward flipped the cell phone around in his right hand and threw it as hard as he could against the window on the passenger's side of his car. He felt a momentary sense of relief, as the phone shattered into hundreds of pieces...but his peace of mind would be short-lived. The reality of the dangerous road ahead quickly grabbed Edward's attention like a stiff drink on a cold winter's night. His eyes became fixated on the curve ahead; however, there was no way he could have ever prepared for what would soon be standing in his way. His body seemed to be frozen in time, while the events started to play out in front of him like a bad dream. Edward's eyes became glued on the set of blue, sparkling lights in the distance...but these were no ordinary lights. The set of lights were, in fact, a pair of bright, blue eyes that seemed to stare directly into his soul, while his body clenched with immediate fear and trepidation. How in the world did that little boy with the red trousers ever end up there? The image of the boy waving his arms got closer and closer to his fast-moving vehicle, and Edward could sense that he had to do something before it was too late. His heart seemed to drop to the floor, as he prepared for the inevitable impact that was staring him in the face. Quickly, Edward realized that he had to swerve to miss the little boy, regardless of what he took out in the process. Edward turned the wheel just as fast as he could, as he slammed on the brakes and closed his eyes. His car bounced off the guard rail and ricocheted off the vehicle that had been resting on the shoulder of the highway, not more than 20 feet from where the little boy was standing. The last thing Edward remembered as his head slammed into the steering wheel was the expression on that little boy's face…he just couldn't shake the look that somehow seemed to be meant for him. Edward simply closed his eyes and presumed that he would never wake up, as he could feel his body getting thrown around his car like a puppet on a string. The car veered off into the center of the highway and began to spin like a top, making seven full turns before it came to rest. The tires of the car were like shredded cheese, and the smell of rubber was everywhere. Edward lay unconscious, while his head came to rest on the shattered dashboard. Slowly, Edward could feel his eyes begin to open, and he felt a stream of blood make a path down the side of his weathered face. Edward reached down toward his bended legs just to make sure they were still attached. He put his hands on his face, frantically searching for his mouth, nose, and lips that had been taken for granted up until now. Edward could feel his pulse begin to slow down, as he realized that everything miraculously seemed to be in place. Edward's body exhaled with a momentary sigh of relief, but his internal peace would be gone in a flash. Reality was about to set in once again, and Edward's decompressed mindset would be here and gone before he knew it. Suddenly, he remembered the look that mesmerized him just seconds before...and the sparkling, blue eyes that met his just prior to the crash. Edward slowly turned the handle on the inside of the door and felt it open, as if to dare him to set foot on the pavement just outside his shattered box of metal.

Edward found himself waiting for something to break, while he tentatively began to stand up. How in the world did he ever survive such a crash, he thought, as he started to think about the surreal events that had just unfolded. Edward made his way to his feet and began to step forward, hoping he could somehow maintain his balance. For a brief moment in time, he actually felt like a person who had been given a new soul, an unlikely second chance at a life gone mad. However, this temporary state of euphoria would quickly dart away, while Edward began to play back the events that had unfolded just moments ago. He turned his head back toward the wreckage passed just seconds before, and he couldn't believe what was staring back his way! The little boy's beautiful, blue eyes were still fixated on his, as Edward felt the salt from his tears play havoc with the cuts that lined his dirty face. He began to move toward the little boy who now stood approximately 50 yards in front of him. The little boy continued to stare back into his eyes, while the two of them got closer and closer to one another. As Edward began to approach the little boy, he couldn't help but notice that the boy was holding onto something in the palm of his tiny, right hand. Slowly, Edward made his way to where the boy was standing, and he knelt down on one knee to see if the little boy was ok. His face had no expression, but his eyes continued to stare into Edward's. Edward reached out his hand, as the little boy dropped the gold chain into the palm of his blackened fingers. Edward looked down at the locket that seemed to be calling out his name…and he slowly opened the latch to see what waited for him on the inside. Without any advanced warning whatsoever, Edward could feel his heart begin to race uncontrollably. As a bead of cold sweat immediately took up residency on his upper lip, he found his eyes captivated by the blue eyes that met his from just inside the locket. The woman on the inside was beautiful, but it was her eyes that immediately grabbed his attention. Where in the world had he seen those beautiful eyes before, he thought, and then it hit him! Edward looked over at the little boy, as tears began to trickle down the side of his red, swollen cheeks. Edward turned back and stared at the mangled car on the side of the road and immediately realized that the little boy was not alone. "No, no, no!" Edward screamed, as he made his way over to the wreckage that lay still in the darkness that surrounded them. Edward crouched down and began to tug on the door, hoping to free whatever it was that waited for him on the other side. His movement seemed to be in slow motion, while he desperately pulled with everything he had left in his body. He felt all of his extremities go numb as his cries echoed in the darkness, almost laughing back at him while he frantically searched for answers. Slowly, the door began to open, and Edward and his little friend looked on. Edward's anticipation was soon overtaken by his worst nightmare, as the woman on the latch stared back at him from the floor of the car. Edward reached down and felt her pulse, hoping that his immediate intuition was wrong. The pulse was silent, and Edward could feel his heart slowly begin to break. As he turned around to find his new-found little friend, he was once again captivated by the boy's blue eyes. However, this time around, his little blue eyes had been converted to red...just like Edward's. The two of them stared out into the darkness but said nothing. Oh, how Edward wanted to somehow find the words that would console his acquaintance, but what in the world could he possibly say? New tears replaced older ones at record pace, as Edward looked on from a distance. Silence gripped the two of them, while the woman in the locket lay motionless just a few feet away. One thing was for certain on this dark, cold night...neither of their lives would ever be the same again.

Chapter Two

The First Wish

The woman looked over at Edward in his cell, as tears began to flow from his eyes. She found herself growing impatient with his emotional state of mind, but she realized that this was something she would need to put up with, at least for now. She also knew that Edward needed to move on and determine what his first wish would be, but first, he had to go back to the image of that little boy…and the woman who was waiting for him as he opened the car door. The woman did, in fact, turn out to be the little boy's mother, which seemed to make matters even worse for Edward. After the authorities had arrived, the little boy was whisked away while Edward looked on from a distance. The little boy never said a word to Edward the entire evening, but Edward would never forget the whimpering sounds that cut through him like a knife. No matter how hard Edward tried to capture the words that would help ease the pain, everything he said and did had zero impact. The empty look that consumed the little boy's face was more than Edward could bear, as he continually played back the events of the night that would haunt him forever. If only he could have that night back once again, he would do so in a heartbeat...

"Mr. Conners, it's time for you to make your first wish. Remember...this wish could allow you to get your life back on track. You have the unique opportunity to make amends for the mistakes of your past, but it all depends on the wish you choose. Do you realize just how lucky you are? Everyone would love to positively influence their past, but you actually have the unique opportunity to do so. The one caveat to your granted wish is that once the change is made, you will now need to live with the decision you have made. Now, what will it be? You have five minutes to make your decision, or you will lose this unique privilege that you've been given." Edward started to think back on the events of his past and found it very difficult to prioritize his personal transgressions. There were things he wished he had done the first time around, but for whatever reason, he wasn't able to pull it off when he originally had the chance. Suddenly, without any advanced warning whatsoever, his conniving mind kicked into high gear. He began to devise a plan that would allow him to win at this game, too, just like he'd done at all the rest. The little boy's face slowly began to fade away from his mind, as Edward thought about the real event that contributed to this mess in the first place. If Andrew Ridgeley III would have made me his executor, Edward thought, then Sylvia would not be in control of my personal finances, and I would have full authority over the personal estate he has left behind. Edward's mind began to race, while he thought about the wish that was now at his fingertips. Edward knew he could influence the events with the little boy if he somehow went upstream and dealt with the real problem at hand. Edward could feel his mind kick into high gear, as he felt a smile begin to form on his tired face. He started to think about how he could get himself out of this predicament, yet still maintain his personal wealth in the process. The thought of slamming Sylvia at the same time made him feel even better about the path he found himself going down. His wish was about to go into effect, and he would be the one who gained the most...just the way he had always wanted it! The sadness of the little boy's face was almost a distant memory for him, as he rationalized his decision moving forward. Edward felt good about the direction he was heading...he had made his decision.

The woman reached her hands into the cell, as Edward slowly met hers just as they entered his new home. Her fingers took on an icy chill, while they formed around their desired target. Edward's body seemed to be hypnotized once again, feeling the woman's presence engulf his every thought. His conscience was warning him that the path he was about to take was a dangerous one, but Edward wasn't listening. For a brief moment in time, he could still remember his mother telling him years ago that all things happen in life for a reason, but Edward wasn't buying this sorry explanation at all. He had only one thing on his mind, and that was to retrieve the life he once knew. After all, the woman who mysteriously made her way into his cell seemed to be looking out for

Edward's best interests, and her offer was about all he had in front of him right now. His life had spiraled out of control, and now he had an opportunity to right the ship. In the process, he would also recover the wealth he so dearly coveted. The woman's scarf still covered her face, but Edward wasn't worrying about his peculiar acquaintance. All he knew was that this woman came out of nowhere with a proposition that could help fix the past, and he wasn't about to test her legitimacy. After all, what was the worst thing that could happen to him right now, he thought, as he began to think through the words that would reflect his first wish. Edward took a deep breath. He was about to request the improbable, before it was too late.

"Ma'am, I do believe I've finalized my decision. Now, let me get this straight. You're giving me the opportunity to make three wishes. The first of these three needs to be finalized right now, the second six months from now, and the third...one year from now, to the day. I assume you'll find me on those dates, and then we'll go through a process similar to tonight? Once I make a wish, it will change that particular event in my life...and my new life will move forward with the change that has been made. Is this correct?" asked Edward, as he looked for clarification from the woman who continued to stare back his way. "Yes, you are correct, Mr. Conners. I will be paying two more visits to you. Each visit will be made in the evening, just like tonight...and the change will go into effect the next morning when you wake up. Now, are you ready to make your decision?" asked the

woman, as she peered into the cell. "Time is running out."
"Yes, I'm ready to make my decision, but I do have one more
question for you. What's in it for you?" inquired Edward, as
he found himself staring at the dark figure once again. "Don't
worry about me, Mr. Conners. In due time, this will all make
sense to you. But until then, you have a very important decision to make. Now, what will it be, Mr. Conners?" Edward
thought back to what he really wanted in life, and the decision was an easy one. "My first wish is that I am named the
immediate beneficiary of Andrew Ridgeley's estate, which
will make me the sole recipient of everything he owned.
I happen to know that he was a lot better off than people
thought he was when he decided to take his own life. He
just got greedy and always wanted more, similar to everyone
else in this world...including me! This means I will have
full control over his business...and his wife, Sylvia, will be
left with absolutely nothing. After the way she's treated me
the past couple of days, I can't wait to pay her another visit."
The woman stared back at Edward and calmly nodded her
head in agreement. "You should try to get some sleep, Mr.
Conners," said the woman, as she pulled away from the cell.
"Your new life begins in the morning."

The woman slowly began to proceed down the hallway
that separated the cells in Block D. Edward watched her
make her way into the distance, until she disappeared around
the turn that extended toward the south end of the building.
Edward began to settle back on to the mattress that rested
near the corner of his cell, when he heard a faint, whis-

tling noise coming from the cell next to his. Edward could not actually see the person disguised as his new next door neighbor, but he distinctly heard the two words that came his way. "Be careful," the voice whispered, as Edward felt his heart begin to race. "Who are you? Did you hear what we were talking about? Why don't you just go back to sleep and mind your own business?" replied Edward. Somehow, he felt violated by the eavesdropping that had just occurred at his expense, even though he knew the words directed toward him may have been warranted. Edward was not in any mood right now to have a reason to question the choice he had just made. How dare this person just sit and listen, and then when it was safe, whisper two words that did nothing but cause further angst and confusion. He waited for an answer to come back his way…but there was nothing. For a brief moment in time, Edward began to wonder if he had made the right decision. After all, he had chosen a path that was solely focused on his personal well-being and nobody else. This was not uncommon for Edward because his life had always been about his own personal advancement. He lay his head down on the pillow, while his eyes continued to stare at the ceiling just above his bed. He found himself focusing on the little, black spec of dirt that rested just above his weary eyes…only to realize that this little spec was slowly moving from right to left just above him. Edward watched as the little bug seemed to be almost tormenting him on its path to the other side of the cell. Slowly, the little, black bug maneuvered its way across the ceiling, only to stop and somehow stare back Edward's way. His mind began to wander, as he thought about the similarities between himself and his new, little cellmate. Neither of them knew for sure what the future would bring, but both felt compelled to keep moving. Sitting still and doing nothing definitely wasn't the answer because this would only add to their own personal vulnerability. Edward watched as the little bug seemed to confuse him even more, and before he knew it, he was fast asleep. The morning would soon arrive, and Edward would be faced with the outcome of the decision he had just made. His first wish was ready to go into effect...

"Mr. Conners, your ride is out front. Bail has been posted for you, so it's time for you to go home now," said Officer Jenkins, as he began to turn the key to the cell. "What in the world are you talking about?" asked Edward, while he slowly made his way to his feet after the first good night's sleep in a very long time. "Last night, you guys wouldn't give me the time of day and now you're letting me out of here. Can you please tell me why the sudden change of heart?" "No problem, Mr. Conners," replied Jenkins. "We've been told that you will no longer be needed here in our jail because we have far better things to do with our time. Bail was posted for you this morning, which means you're no longer required to stay. I hope you have a great rest of the day, sir. The weather is absolutely perfect out there. Please, let us know if you need anything at all." Edward slowly made his way out of the cell and shook his head, confused and bewildered as to how things did an about face so quickly. He turned around and took one final glance at the cell he was leaving behind, almost in disbelief that this was his home for the past three days. Just as Edward began to turn and walk toward the entrance of Block D, he remembered the voice that came his way from the night before. The words "be careful" were embedded in his mind, as he turned back toward the cell that was responsible for the voice from the dark. This was where the whisper had come from the night before, and Edward found himself racing to identify the source. He started back toward the darkened room, while Jenkins watched from afar. Jenkins couldn't help but wonder why Edward wasn't sprinting out of the jail at a time like this, just like so many others he had watched over the years. Why was he so enamored with the cell next to his, Jenkins thought, as he watched Edward stare into the room surrounded by bars. "Can I help you with something, Mr. Conners?" asked Officer Jenkins. "Is there anyone staying in this cell, officer?" responded Edward, still remembering the words that came his way less than 12 hours before. "Mr. Conners, the old guy who was in this cell was moved to another area of the prison," replied Jenkins. "He's had real bad health issues, and we needed to move him to another wing so he could get the help he needed. He's going to be just fine. We try to make sure we always take good care of our inmates here. Why...did you know him, sir?" "Nope, I never met him," responded Edward. "Hopefully, I never will now. Let's get out of here, officer." "Sounds good to me," responded Officer Jenkins. "Your ride is waiting out front."

Edward made his way down the sidewalk and immediately became fixated on the limousine that was parked
directly across the street. The window slowly opened, and
Edward could hear the voice that was directed his way.
"Get in the car, Mr. Conners. We have a lot of work to do."
Edward moved closer and closer to the open door and, before
he knew it, he was seated next to the voice that had called
out his name just moments before. Edward looked over at
the man who was seated next to him; however, he had no
idea who the man was...he had never seen him before in
his life. "Who are you?" asked Edward, as he felt his heart
almost skip a beat while staring over at his newly discovered
acquaintance. "Edward, I'm your new counselor. Granted...
you're a terrific lawyer yourself, but I am simply the best.
I'll be representing you in your upcoming trial, which will
be unlike anything you've ever been through before. You're
about to find out firsthand just how difficult it is to be on the
receiving end of the barbs and innuendos that will be coming
your way. I'll be there to deflect the arrows that are meant
for you, but we will need to move quickly. Your life will be
on the line, so it will be critical that we develop our strategy
right now. We need to get over to my office and get started.
Oh, by the way, my name is Warren Mize. Hey, Thomas,
let's get out of here. This place is making me sick to my
stomach." With that, the car sped out of the parking spot and
quickly made its way down the city's main thoroughfare.

Edward was speechless. He looked over at the graying
gentleman with dark, brown circles under his eyes and simply

shook his head in agreement. Edward's mind began to move back in time, while he methodically replayed the events of the past three days. His life had gone through numerous contortions, none of them making any sense whatsoever. First, Ridgeley kills himself by crashing his car into the tree. Shortly after the crash, Sylvia fires Edward and even calls him back to inflict additional pain, gloating the entire time at his expense. Then, Edward finds himself spinning out of control, just missing a little boy standing on the side of the road. And then to top it off…the little boy proceeds to give Edward a locket with a picture of a woman who Edward finds in the car…dead! Before Edward knows it, he finds himself in a jail cell making a deal with a creepy, old lady…and then he ends up in a limo with a man who goes on to tell him that he will be representing him in his trial. Wait just a minute, Edward thought, as he tried desperately to make sense out of a life that was officially moving at warp speed…and none of it very good right now! Edward had heard enough. He needed to get some answers…

"Pull the car over right now," shouted Edward, as he stared over at Mize. "I have no idea who you are and what you think you're doing. I need answers from you before we go any further, Mize. You need to start from the beginning, and then I'll tell you if you're going to be my counselor or not. You're not calling the shots here…I am! Do you under-stand what I'm saying?" Mize took a deep breath, as he felt the blood start to rush to his forehead. Oh, how he wanted to take this man apart, but for now, he would placate Edward's desire to be in control. This was hard for Mize to do, but he knew his subservient position would only be temporary. Soon, he would be in full control of the situation once again. But for now, he would play this silly game with Edward. After all, he was the client. "Edward, slow down. Let me make this as clear as possible. Ridgeley's decision to make you the prime beneficiary after his passing made you one of the richest men in the entire area, but with this wealth comes a price to pay. You need to be very aggressive in your defense, or you'll lose everything. When you swerved to miss that little boy, you wiped out the car he was in just moments before. We need to be very careful regarding the position we pursue, which means we will take no prisoners during the process. I've never lost a case like this, and trust me, I've been involved in more of these than anyone else in this county. As you well know, the public's interest in a case like this is multiplied tenfold when there is a lot of money at stake. You knew all along that Ridgeley's financial picture was much better than anyone ever imagined. In fact, rumor has it that his suicide had nothing at all to do with any financial difficulties whatsoever. Ridgeley was a smart man when it came to his finances, and he totally bluffed his wife into thinking that his decision to hit that tree was based strictly on his perceived financial decimation. His suicide had been in the works for a long time, and that tree provided him with an easy way out. Someday, it will all come out, but all you need to know right now is that you've been given the keys to his $10M portfolio. This means you need to protect it with your life....or it will be taken away in a flash. Our first action item is this trial. We need to get you off that manslaughter charge and then you can move on with your life. I'm here to help you. And trust me when I say this...you need my help right now. You really have nobody else."

Edward took a deep breath and reluctantly reached out to shake Mize's weathered, right hand. Mize smiled and then tapped Thomas on the shoulder. "Be careful up here, Thomas," said Mize. "Go around the back of the building. I want to make sure nobody is watching us right now. I don't want anyone to know that I'm representing Edward because the word will spread quickly, and then we will be hounded by the press no matter what we do. I don't want anyone to know we're a team until we absolutely have to tell them. Since Edward was named as the head of Ridgeley's estate, this will create nothing but questions and incessant badgering by the press. We need to catch the prosecution off guard, creating a false sense of security for them along the way. As soon as they find out I'm involved, they'll put their game face on because they know they'll be in for a fight. I want to get a head start on them beginning right now. Our trial will be starting in the fall, which gives us just under six months to get ready. This is not a lot of time, Edward. Your life will be hanging in the balance, so we need to get everything in place. You and I are going to eat and breathe this trial over the next six months, and no rock will go unturned." Edward looked over at Mize and could immediately tell that he was truly in his element. Mize was back in control, and Edward would be following his lead. He looked over at Edward, as a slight grin began to form on his face. One thing was for certain...Edward's first wish was now in full motion.

Chapter Three

Payback

T he woman made her way down the dark alley and slowly moved toward the small cottage at the end of the cobblestone walk. Her fingers reached up and entered the code that would unlock the door, allowing her entry into the room that awaited her. She was the last of the participants on this particular evening; however, her feedback would be the primary reason for the committee's Tuesday night gathering. Silence filled the room as Celeste made her way in, nodding to the whites of the eyes that circled the ring meant for her. In the middle of the room was her chair because tonight her testimony would be on display for all to see. Celeste sat down in the chair and waited for the questions that would soon come her way. "So, Celeste, how did it go with Mr. Conners last night? I assume everything is right on target, according to our plans?" asked the voice from behind the platform that extended above the ring of participants. The face was unrecognizable due to the darkness, but the voice was undeniably that of their leader. "Everything is right on target, sir," responded Celeste. "Mr. Conners had his first wish granted, and our plan has officially been put into motion. Our initial impression of Mr. Conners was accurate, as his love of money and power will play right into our trap. I'm confident our ultimate objective will be met." "Good work, Celeste. I don't need to remind you just how important this assignment is regarding your future well-being. My only recommendation to you at this juncture is that you take nothing for granted. The events that are in front of us are only a means to our ends. Our ultimate goal, which is how you will be evaluated when all is said and done, has only one metric of measurement...and all of us here know what this means now, don't we? Do I make myself clear, Celeste?" "Yes, sir. I will keep a close eye on Mr. Conners and report anything back to you that contradicts our plans. However, I'm confident there will be nothing out of the ordinary to bring back to the team," said Celeste, as she looked out at the numerous sets of eyes that stared back at her in the center of the room. "For your sake, I hope you're right, Celeste. You may go now," responded the raspy voice from just outside her view. With that, Celeste made her way to the door and proceeded to show her way out. Never looking back, she knew she was being watched by all. As she closed the door behind her, she could feel the perspiration slowly drip down the side of her face. Her entire future depended on a positive outcome regarding Edward Conners, and she knew it. Facing the committee with anything less than the feedback they wanted to hear was something she didn't even want to think about right now. She made her way down the walkway and back into the darkened alley, never looking back. She was glad to be leaving for now, but she knew her reprieve from the committee would be short-lived. There would be a time that her presence would be required once again, but until then, she would somehow try to get on with her life.

Mize and Thomas whisked Edward out of the limousine, as they proceeded to move through the back door of the office building that awaited them. Mize entered through the darkened entrance with Edward not far behind. Thomas protected the two of them from the rear and watched intently to make sure they were not seen. Quickly, they made their way through the quiet corridor that led to Mize's office at the corner of the hallway. Within minutes, the three of them were inside as they followed Mize into the boardroom just adjacent to his office. Mize immediately mapped out a flow-chart that summarized the details leading up to the event in question. He looked over at Edward and began the dialogue that had been building up for quite some time. "Edward, we need to go over every single detail leading up to the crash," stated Mize, as he made his way over to where Edward was already sitting. "I've tried to capture the general events as I know them, but I have no doubt in my mind that I'm missing critical elements of the night in question. This is where I'm going to need your help. We can't leave anything uncovered or we both know what will happen. I realize that you're very familiar with the courtroom, Edward, but I need you to promise me one thing. I'm the one calling the shots here. No matter how much you want to take control of this situation,

I need you to follow my lead. We will win this case if we work together as a team...but it won't be easy. We need to find something that will catch the prosecution off guard, and that is why we will review everything from start to finish. You need to check your ego at the door because there will be no place for it in my court of law. No matter what we need to do, we're going to find a way to win this case. Trust me, Edward, the lifestyle you've come to relish depends on it. I know you enjoy the comforts of what wealth can bring; therefore, you need to realize very quickly that your personal portfolio will be the target of the prosecution. We're going to need to make sure that we present you in the right light when it comes to jury perception. The district attorney is going to try to take you down, and that's why I'm here. My job is to make sure this doesn't happen. I also need you to grasp one very important concept when it comes to my philosophy about the court of law. I'm not interested in the truth. I'm only interested in one thing...and that is winning. Do I make myself clear? This is all I care about regarding any of my cases, including yours." Edward looked over at Mize and, for a brief moment, he felt the magnitude of what was in front of him. His life truly was hanging in the balance, but he knew he was in good hands with Mize. "Edward, I asked you a question. Do I make myself clear?" asked Mize, as he stared back at Edward from the flowchart at the front of the room. "Mize, don't worry about me," snapped Edward, while he could feel his role as Mize's puppet begin to take hold. "You know I'm in, and I will follow your lead." Mize had Edward right where he wanted him, while he nodded his head in agreement. He was in his element now, and without any doubt whatsoever, he would be the one calling all the shots from this point forward.

Since this was the highest profile case ever seen in Epoch County, Jacob Hearn had come to the realization that their new district attorney would undoubtedly be impacting his political future in a significant way. Rumor had spread that Jacob was far too soft for his position, and many in the area believed that changes needed to be made in order for the city to move forward. He could ill afford another setback, as his re-election bid as the mayor of Cradle Ridge was now hanging in the balance. This case would cement his legacy one way or the other, and the press had already started to gather near the steps of the courthouse. Rumblings that Edward Conners would soon be facing the trial of his life had stirred up the locals and many in the area were "chompin' at the bit" to get a piece of the action. The events over the past week had been a whirlwind for everyone involved, and Jacob was beginning to feel the pressure of the case grab hold of him like flypaper on a hot summer's day. He shook his head in disbelief, while he stared down at the name of the newly hired prosecuting attorney. How in the world did Abby Holt ever get this position, Jacob thought, as he felt his mind drift back to the name he wanted to see rather than hers. Why did the city's old veteran, Ben Joulson, have to retire last month and give way to this rookie, barely out of law school? Jacob begrudgingly allowed his mind to wander back to the day

Abby first arrived, as his initial impression of her wasn't a very good one. She seemed to be highly determined to get her own way, which was a total dichotomy to her predecessor. Ben's methodical ways had been a good fit for the city, but then again, Cradle Ridge had never seen a case quite like this one. Jacob reached for his phone and began to dial her number. He needed to make sure his position regarding this case was crystal clear. "Hello, this is Abby Holt, what can I do for you?" answered the voice on the other end of the line. Oh, how Jacob wished for Ben's voice instead, but he knew Ben's days were a thing of the past. He was, in fact, stuck with this new girl…whether he liked it or not! Jacob knew he had to find a way to mesh with her personality because she wasn't going anywhere, and she certainly wasn't about to change.

Sylvia shook her head in disbelief, as she continued to question the papers that lay in front of her, almost laughing in her face. How in the world did she miss the fine print that accompanied the estate? She just assumed that her husband of 22 years would leave everything for her, but this careless mistake would be a costly one as she contemplated her next move. "Clark Davis, are you sure about this? How could Andrew do this to me? I was told that everything was mine, and now you're dropping this bomb at my feet. How could he possibly have snuck this by me? You've been a trusted friend of our family for years, and now you're telling me that the entire estate is being handed over to my greatest nemesis of all, Edward Conners!" screamed Sylvia, as she felt the life she so desperately coveted quickly leave her grasp. Without any advanced warning, the office door opened…which was not a good thing for the uninvited guest who dared to enter. "Maria, you get out of here right now!" shouted Sylvia, as she turned toward their maidservant in charge. "How dare you barge in here when you know I'm in the middle of a meeting!" "I am so sorry, ma'am," responded Maria. "I had no idea you were in here." In the nick of time, Clark intervened and Sylvia's attention was once again on the papers that rested in front of her. "Mrs. Ridgeley, sit down and let me explain this to you. There was an addendum to your trust that you personally signed last year. I can't be blamed for your unwillingness to read the fine print in the addendum. Your husband and I drafted this addendum, and he told me that he had you sign it. My job was not to question him, but only to draw up the estate, including any provisions, to meet his specifications. Is this not your signature here at the bottom of the last page?" inquired Clark, as he handed the papers back to Sylvia. "Yes, this is my signature! But I didn't think it was necessary for me to read every single word in this stupid document. Andrew just told me that I needed to sign it so we had everything in place in case something ever happened to him. He told me that he was adding a few more of our assets to the trust, but he never said a word about including Conners as the beneficiary. Why didn't you tell me about this, Clark? You've always been a trusted friend… you knew all along that Conners was getting everything, didn't you? This is all your fault!" Clark reached back across the table and picked up the scattered papers. He gathered the documents and put them back into his briefcase, as he looked back at Sylvia with her head buried between her arms on the table. "Mrs. Ridgeley, I'm sorry you feel this way, but your husband made it very clear to me that the two of you had discussed this addendum at length. My job was to follow his instructions. Good-bye ma'am...I really am sorry you feel the way you do, but there's nothing I can do right now. I wish you the best."

Silence filled the room, as Sylvia began to feel the reality of the situation squeeze her like a vice. How could everything change so quickly, she thought, as her mind was now moving at record pace. In less than a week, she not only lost her husband...but the lifestyle that went along with him as well. It was hard for her to decide which loss hurt the most, as she began to think about the lavish hotels and restaurants that had become a vital part of her life. Slowly, her mind began to drift off, only to be interrupted by the ringing of the cell phone lying next to her. The pulsating vibrations seemed to be calling out her name. Maybe, just maybe, Clark was calling back to apologize and everything would get back to normal once again. Sylvia could feel a smile slowly begin to form on her face, while she allowed her mind to wander back to years gone by. Oh, how she hoped this would be the call she longed for, the call she so desperately needed right now. Just maybe... her nightmare would soon end and life would be back to the way it was before Andrew's untimely departure. Unfortunately for Sylvia, this would not be the case, as she reached for the phone that would quickly bring her back to reality. There was no way Sylvia could have ever prepared for the voice that eagerly awaited hers. The sound on the other end of the phone was a familiar one, but the tone would be much different than the last conversation that took place.

"Hello, this is Sylvia Ridgeley, can I help you?" answered Sylvia, while she began to settle back down into her seat. Laughter was all that awaited her, and she felt hypnotized by the rhythmic noises that were undoubtedly directed her way. "Who is this?" asked Sylvia, as her pulse began to pick up speed with every chuckle that methodically pierced her ears. "I don't find this amusing at all," said Sylvia, "you must have the wrong number. And don't you ever call back here again!" "Wait just a minute," responded the voice. "This is an old friend of yours. I'm sorry I started to laugh at you, but it's just that I find this call so incredibly amusing. As a matter of fact, I'm pinching myself right now just to make sure this isn't a dream. Because if it's a dream, I do know one thing is for sure. I never, ever want to wake up! Do you have any idea who this is, Sylvia?" asked the voice that slowly began to regain temporary composure at Sylvia's expense. "I don't know who this is, you fool, and I really don't care," screamed Sylvia. "Now, if you don't mind, I don't want you to ever call back here again. I don't appreciate you interrupting my evening one bit." The voice on the other end of the line wasn't through just yet...his gauntlet was about to be dropped! "I totally understand, princess, and I promise I will never call you back again. In fact, I have no reason to speak with you after tonight, but I do have one more thing to say to you. Edward Conners sends his best...good night, Sylvia."

Sylvia's jaw dropped, while she felt the magnitude of the message kick her squarely in the gut. Edward, on the other hand, just sat and smiled. He savored the thought of what had just transpired and wished he could see Sylvia's face right now. Finally, Sylvia had been put in her place, and the idea of her on the receiving end of his message made the turn of events even sweeter than he ever imagined. Edward just sat and closed his eyes. If only he could relish this personal victory forever. For the first time in over a week, he actually felt a smile totally consume his face. Unfortunately for Edward, his personal victory would be short-lived. The jaws of reality would soon be sinking their teeth into him once again...

Chapter Four

The Dream

Abby closed her eyes and could see her father staring back at her, just like he did numerous times when she was a young girl back in Idaho. His dark, brown eyes had always been there for her, as the life they had been given made it nearly impossible for it to be any other way. It had been almost 25 years since the night that changed everything for the two of them, but on this particular evening, it seemed like it was just yesterday. She had done a good job of moving on with her life, but tonight the past would be knocking on her door, begging for entry. This would be one of those nights when the knocks would be answered, and her past would be taking up residency in her mind all over again. Within seconds, she found herself back in Idaho...where life was simple and beautiful. This was the part of the dream that Abby longed for the most, the part she wished would never end. If only it was that easy, she would make it a point to visit this dream every night. However, this peaceful beginning of her dream would quickly change, and her daddy's brown eyes would be needed more than ever before...

"Mama, why do we need to go to Gram's house again this Christmas?" asked Abby, as she brushed her seven-year-old locks with the fervor of a thoroughbred trainer before a big race. "Why can't Gram ever come here for Christmas? I get real nervous that Santa may forget about Emma and me at her house, and one of these days, we just might not have any presents there. Can't we just have Gram come to our house this year so we know for sure the presents will be here?" "Now, Abby, you know Santa isn't going to forget you and your sister on Christmas Day," responded Abby's mother, Nancy, while she looked over at her oldest daughter. "Gram is getting way too old to make the drive back here to Idaho. We need to go see her so she isn't home alone. Plus, you and your sister love it in Montana at Christmas time. Don't you want to go visit her and go sleigh riding and build snow angels like you always do? You know how much Gram loves having you and Emma there this time of year. We'll make sure Santa doesn't forget the two of you, ok? Your father and I will never let that happen. I promise." Abby looked over at her mom and smiled. No matter how scary the situation was, her mother always said the right thing. Today would be no different. In the blink of an eye, Gram's house in Montana seemed like the perfect place to be at Christmas time. Abby and her little sister, Emma, would soon be making gingerbread houses at Gram's house, and life would be perfect once again.

William and Nancy packed the car with everything they would need in order to make the trip; however, this year's journey seemed to reflect a much larger load than in the past. The girls were getting older and their expanded wardrobes were beginning to reflect this change as well. The trip seemed to be getting longer every year as well, and all William could think of was how nice it would be to simply relax in the confines of his own home at Christmas time. He also knew that his mother-in-law's health was deteriorating rapidly, and their trips to Montana would soon be coming to an end. William had become a master at dealing with winter roads, but this year's forecast was even more concerning to him due to the ice that was heading their way. "Honey, let's try to get out of here as early as possible tomorrow," said William, as he closed up his last suitcase before calling it a night. "There's supposed to be a major storm moving into Montana late tomorrow afternoon, and I really want to be there before the bad stuff hits." "Sounds like a plan, dear, but I don't think I'm the one you need to convince," responded Nancy, as she looked over at William and smiled. "Getting the girls up early is our major challenge every year. You'd think we'd be getting better at these trips with all our practice, but it doesn't seem like we're improving at all." "You're right...we'll just do our best and take it easy on our way," said William, as he smiled back at the woman he fell in love with many years ago. "Driving with you and the girls is much different than when I tackle these trips alone. I just don't want to take any chances. We'll find a way to deal with the elements like we always do and it'll work out. It always does." Nancy nodded her head in agreement, while she watched her husband of 14 years call it a night. On evenings like these, she realized just how blessed she really was…and how much her family truly meant to her.

Abby tossed and turned, as her dream began to pick up speed. This was the part of her dream that she hated the most, the part that would change her life forever. No matter how hard she tried to erase the events that raced toward her like a runaway locomotive, there was no way she could shake the outcome she dreaded the most. Oh, how Abby wanted to stop right here and rewrite the ending to her dream…but it just wasn't possible. She closed her eyes as tight as she could, hoping that when they opened, everything would go back to her simple life in Idaho. The life she cherished with all her heart was about to be turned upside down in a matter of minutes, and the outcome for everyone involved would be permanent. Abby's life in Idaho was nothing more than a distant memory, as she prepared herself for the inevitable outcome that would be coming her way…

Abby was seated directly behind her father in the back seat of their blue sedan, as the snow was beginning to fall at record pace. "I think I'm going to need to find a place for us to stay tonight," said William, as he glanced over at Nancy on the passenger's side of their car. "I'm having a very difficult time seeing the road, and we still have at least three hours before we reach your mom's place. I just don't want to risk it. Is that ok, honey?" "No problem, William, I agree. I'm having all kinds of trouble seeing anything myself," responded Nancy, knowing full well that the storm was here to stay for quite some time. Abby looked over at her little sister, Emma, who was sleeping in the seat right next to her. Oh, how beautiful she was, Abby thought, while her eyes began to slowly move toward the front seat where mom was sitting. Abby could still hear her mother mouth the words, "I'm fine with stopping, sweetheart. We'll make it a fun night." Abby could feel a smile start to form on her face, as she watched her mom and dad from afar. This would be the last time her smile would have the same meaning...it was about to be changed forever.

Out of nowhere came two, bright headlights from the right, as Abby looked over in shock and disbelief. Without any warning whatsoever, the lights buried themselves into the right side of the sedan with intense force, only to be followed up by the direct impact of the semi-trailer that was close behind. Nancy and Emma took the brunt of the force, as the massive box of metal buried its teeth into the side of their car with no regard for anything that stood in its way. The sedan crumbled like a deck of cards, and the driver could do nothing to slow down its deadly path. For nearly 20 seconds, the semi and sedan were connected as one...and then silence filled the air with the remnants of just how fragile life can really be. As it would turn out, Gerald Pressley, the driver of the semi, would never be the same again. Although he would survive the crash, the haunting memories of that cold, December night would never go away...and he would die four years later of a broken heart. After the crash, Abby would remember nothing except the nurse who would be waiting for her when her eyes eventually opened. 57 days in a coma would finally come to an end, but the news that would soon come her way would rock her world forever.

"Abby, my name is Carolyne, and I'm a nurse here at the Onicerra Trauma Center. You've been here for a very long time, Abby, and now you're going to need your rest. I know you have a lot of questions, and I'll be here to help you... but right now, please get some sleep, ok? You're an amazing young girl, and I am so proud of you," said the seasoned nurse who hadn't missed a day since Abby first arrived. Abby looked up at her newfound friend and cracked a small smile, while her eyes slowly began to close once again. Carolyne turned her head away, as she felt her pulse begin to race. Closing her eyes and lifting her head up toward the sky, she could feel God's presence immediately engulf the room. The fact that Abby had opened her eyes after the injuries she sustained was truly a miracle. But...Carolyne also knew her road to recovery would be an incredibly rough one moving forward. Her greatest challenge would not be physical, but instead would entail the mental anguish that was about to come her way. Carolyne could feel a small sigh of relief consume her because she knew Abby would not be alone in her fight. Her father, William, would be there for her as well... and Carolyne couldn't wait to give him the incredible news!

"Mr. Holt, I need to talk with you about something," said Carolyne, as she quickly made her way down the hallway to William's room. "I need you to promise me one thing. We're at a very critical juncture right now, and I need you to follow my lead regarding next steps, ok? Our timing needs to be perfect because the news I'm about to share with you must be handled delicately...no matter how much you want to move on it right away." William could feel his eyes begin to well up with tears because he could sense for the first time in two months that the news heading his way would finally be positive. "Mr. Holt, Abby is beginning to come out of her coma. She just responded to me a short while ago, and now her recovery team is in the room with her checking all of her vitals. I've been here since she was first brought in, and I know what a blessing this is to all of us, especially you. I've worked at this trauma center for over 20 years, and I've never had a patient fight as hard as your daughter. I truly believe that God has an amazing plan for her life, but we need to realize that we aren't out of the woods just yet. There are a number of very difficult days still in front of us, and this is where I'm really going to need your help. Our immediate reaction is to get in there and hold her tight and just love on her like never before, but we need to be very careful about how we handle the next couple of days. She has no idea what happened after the crash, and I'm sure she will be asking all of us a lot of questions very soon. I do believe that your time with her when she wakes up will be something that only you can prepare for, and you have my word that nobody will speak with Abby before you do about the outcome of the crash. I've spoken to Dr. Gould and he agrees with me that any communication about the event needs to come from you, but we need to make sure Abby is ready. Mr.

Holt, is this ok with you? If you want me to help out in any way, I will be here for you." William began to sob uncontrollably, as he reached out for Carolyne's hands. "Thank you, thank you," cried William, as he felt tears release down both sides of his tired face. "As soon as I can see my Abby, please let me know, ok? I need her more than ever right now, but I want to make sure she's ready. I'll wait for you to give me the word. I have total trust in you and the rest of the staff." Carolyne nodded her head in agreement, as she turned and made her way out the door. All William could do was bury his head in his pillow and thank God for the gift he had been given. His personal faith over the past two months had been shaken...but he had never given up hope that Abby would make it. Now, his prayers would be focused on not only his daughter's recovery, but on his own personal strength as well. William knew Abby would need him more than ever before, and that he would play a critical role in her recovery process. There was no way she could ever get through the coming days alone.

"Edward, we need to go back and retrace your steps regarding the evening in question," shouted Mize, while he continued to review his pages of notes. "You need to think back on every little detail you can remember because we can't afford to miss anything. Let's go back to when you left the office on the day of Ridgeley's death. Now, take me through the sequence of events once again." "Come on, Mize, we've gone over this before. I told you I left the office and then the phone rang," responded Edward. "I answered the phone and it was Ridgeley's wife, Sylvia. She and I've always had a bad taste for one another, and this night would be no different. She proceeded to tell me that I was fired as their counselor due to Andrew's death. She made it very clear that I wasn't needed anymore, and that she'd been looking forward to this day for a very long time. In fact, I got the impression that her happiness in firing me was far greater than her sadness in losing her husband. Within a couple of minutes on the phone, she fired me, and I was done. Then, as if her teeth hadn't sunk into me quite deep enough yet, she called back for more. My phone rang a second time, and it was Sylvia, eagerly awaiting her opportunity to inflict even more salt to the wound. She then told me that I needed to return the car as well because this was a part of my termination, which really set me off. That's when I threw my phone against the passenger window. Without any warning whatsoever, I looked up and saw a little boy standing on the side of the road. I have no idea where he came from, but he was there staring at me while my car moved closer and closer to where he was standing. He didn't move, and before I knew it, I was within a few yards of wiping him out. At the very last second, I veered off to the side of the road and crashed into the car that was parked near where he was standing. My car ricocheted off the parked car, and then I went into a spin. This is where it gets a little bit fuzzy for me. After my car stopped, I had no idea what damage had been done, and I did my best to make sure all of my limbs were still in place. I remember trying to get out of the car, totally dazed and confused. Once I got my bearings, I looked back toward the wreckage behind me. Standing next to the pile of rubble was the little boy, still staring back at me. I don't think he moved at all during the crash because he seemed to be in the exact same spot as when I first laid eyes on him. I made my way over to the car to make sure he was ok, but he said nothing. He just kept staring at me. Tears were rolling down his face, as he dropped a locket into my outstretched hand. I opened the lid of the locket, and there was a picture of a beautiful woman on the inside. I looked back at the car and had a sick feeling in my stomach that the little boy wasn't alone. I ran back to the car and that is when I found the woman lying on the floor of the car. The little boy watched from a distance, as I checked her pulse to see if she was still alive. There was nothing. I looked over at the little boy and the two of us stood motionless, saying nothing to one another. I don't know why I didn't reach out to him to try and console him, but I felt paralyzed. Maybe I was in shock, or afraid…or a little of both, but there just wasn't anything that could take away the pain. I could see it on his face, and I felt like I was going to throw up." Mize looked over at Edward, as tears filled Edward's eyes once again. This was good, Mize thought, as he continued to scribble the notes on his pad. Edward looked over at Mize, hoping for some feedback regarding the information he just provided…but Mize said nothing. The sound of his pen scribbling on the pad echoed in the room, as silence filled the air. Slowly, Mize looked up at Edward, while his hand methodically rubbed the bottom of his chin. His plan was about to go into action. "We need to find that boy," uttered

Mize, as he stared back at Edward, "before the prosecution does. That's my primary concern right now!" Thomas looked on from the back of the room and smiled. Mize was the best at what he did, and he would take out anything, or anybody, who happened to be in his path.

Carolyne made her way into William's room and prepared herself for the news she had been waiting to deliver, as the time had finally come for him to see his daughter. There was no way William could have ever prepared for the conversation that awaited him, but Carolyne had a peace that he would somehow find a way to say the right thing. Abby had been through a lot, but her toughest test would still be in front of her, and Carolyne knew it. "Mr. Holt, how are you feeling this morning?" asked Carolyne, as she reached over and adjusted his pillow. "Good morning, Carolyne. I'm feeling better this morning. I finally had a decent sleep last night. I'm still very sore, but I know the physical pain will go away in due time," responded William. "Well, today is the day we've been waiting for," said Carolyne. "I just stopped by Abby's room, and she's awake. You need to be prepared for what you're about to see, Mr. Holt. Remember...she's been in a coma for almost two months, and her body will be going through a major recovery process in the coming days. She also has very little recollection of what happened on the night of the crash. I'm not going to tell you what to say, but I do want you to know that I've been praying for you. I have a peace that God will put the words in your heart, Mr. Holt, and that He will give you the strength to say the right thing.

Please, let me know if you need me at all. I'll be right down the hallway, ok?" William looked over at Carolyne and nodded his head in agreement. "Thanks, Carolyne. I can't tell you how much your words mean to me right now. I also know that you're one of the primary reasons that my little girl is still with us. I may be taking you up on your offer as we move forward. Let's go…I'm ready to see my little girl."

William moved closer and closer toward the door. He knew Abby was inside waiting for him, and as a result, he felt his heart race and his hands begin to shake. How in the world was he going to handle the next five minutes? He would be delivering the most difficult message of his lifetime, and his little girl would never be the same again after what he was about to tell her. He took a deep breath and looked up at Carolyne, while he tried to capture some much-needed encouragement at her expense. Nodding his head as their eyes met, he reached for the latch that would open the door. Slowly, the door opened and there was Abby, resting on her back with her eyes closed. For a brief moment, William could feel his stomach start to turn, and he felt like he was going to pass out. Abby's head was completely bandaged, except for her eyes, nose, and lips. In order to protect her wounds from infection, the dressing needed to be changed daily. Fortunately for William, he was the recipient of the new gauze, which was a whole lot easier to stomach than what would have awaited him just minutes before. There was still considerable drainage from the injuries she sustained on the night that would change her life forever, but it was the emotional scars that would undoubtedly take the greatest toll on her. William maneuvered his wheelchair so he could get closer to his beautiful, little angel and waited for her eyes to open. Before he got started with the conversation that had played tricks with his mind for days now, all he wanted to do was just stare at her. His little girl was so beautiful …and she was all he had right now. As William reached out and touched her little fingers, he could feel his heart connect with hers as his eyes began to fill with tears. Oh, how William wanted to just lie down next to her and cry, but he knew deep down inside that she would need him more than ever. Quickly, he wiped the tears away and prayed for strength. Abby's eyes started to open and there was William waiting for her, which was exactly what she needed right now. Abby looked up at William and whispered, "Daddy, thanks for being here. I love you…where's Mommy and Emma?" William took a deep breath and whispered, "I love you, too, sweetheart. I'll always be here for you. I need to talk with you about Mommy and Emma. I really don't know how to say this, honey, but I've prayed that God will somehow give me the strength to get through this for you. Two months ago, the four of us were going to Gram's house for Christmas in Montana, just like we do every year. We hit a very bad storm along the way, and the visibility was almost zero. Your mother and I decided to find a place to stay because of the awful conditions. That is when the accident took place. There was a truck that came out of nowhere and went through a stop sign. The driver went on to say that he didn't see the sign, and within seconds, he hit us full force on the passenger side of the car. Mommy and Emma were on that side of the car when he hit us. Abby, sweetheart... Mommy and Emma will not be coming back to be with us anymore. They're in heaven right now. Please, honey, know that I'm here for you. I'm not going anywhere, and I promise I'll always take care of you. We're both going to need each other more than ever before because we're both hurting real bad. I'm so grateful that you're here with me. I love you very, very much." Abby looked up at her father and could say nothing. She closed her eyes, while tears began to flow in and out of the bandages that lined her swollen face. William put his arms around her and held on as tight as he could. The pain of her father's message would never leave her, but Abby would find a way to move on. Somehow, she would funnel all of her emotions into everything she did from this point forward, and she would never forget the love she had for her mother and sister. No matter how difficult her life would be without the two of them, she knew they would want her to go on and fight the fight. Deep down inside, Abby knew they wouldn't want it any other way.

Chapter Five

The Disappearance

"Edward, we've finally located the kid," said Mize, as he looked over at his client's tired face. "Turns out that after the crash, he was taken into protective custody due to the events of the evening in question. You'd think we were trying to locate the president based on the difficulty of nailing this kid down, but it looks like he's over in Landersville. I've got some experience with the folks over there, but quite honestly, they can be a real pain to deal with. We need to get some time with the kid before the trail, but it's going to be tough. The kid's feedback could have a huge impact on the outcome of the trial, and it'll be important for us to have a clear understanding of the role he's going to play. You need to make sure you're not missing anything regarding what he was doing there, and if he said or did anything after the crash that could help us with our case. Now, take me back to what you saw when you first laid eyes on the boy. You mentioned that you noticed him shortly before the crash, and then again after you hit the car he was standing next to. It's almost hard to believe that this kid didn't reveal anything to you…other than crying a few tears, he didn't scream or cry? Are you sure about this, Edward? I've told you from the very start that I don't like surprises of any kind when I get into the courtroom. I've done a lot of homework on the prosecuting attorney, and it looks like she's not going to be any problem at all. She's just a kid out of law school, looking to make a name for herself. We both know that's not going to happen with me in the courtroom. Ben Joulson was a decent guy and I've known him for years, but he decided to retire and move on. He was a good, old boy and never imposed much of a threat to any of my clients, so I'm not too worried about the young lady who took his place. If she's anything like her predecessor, we should be just fine. I'm sure she will be similar to all the other new attorneys that have taken similar jobs in the past. She's going to be scared to death of me when we enter the courtroom, but we still need to be deliberate in our execution of the plan. Edward, take me back to the little boy and share everything you remember about the kid." "Mize, I told you," replied Edward. "The boy was standing next to the parked car when I first saw him. I was moving quickly toward him, and that's when I swerved to miss him. He was just your typical kid. Not much out of the ordinary, but I noticed right away that he stared at me with a look that you don't often see in kids his age. Even after the car came to a stop, he continued to watch me as I got out of my vehicle. When I made it over to him, he gave me the locket with the picture in it. At the time, he didn't say the woman in the car was his mother, but I knew he wasn't alone. I ran to the car, he followed me, and he stood next to me as I checked the woman's pulse. He could tell by my reaction that she was dead. He and I both stood there and didn't say much of anything at all. I think he may have been in shock...and maybe I was as well. Within a few minutes, the medics arrived, and he was quickly whisked off in a car. I haven't seen him since, but I think about him often. In fact, I can't get the kid out of my mind."

"Well, that's all touching and everything, Edward, but quite honestly, I don't care about what you've been thinking!" screamed Mize. "I'm convinced that this kid may know a lot more than what he's saying, and I want to get to him before our day in court. Did you forget that our trial starts in less than two weeks, and we know nothing about one of the most important pieces of this puzzle! I'm going to reach out to the prosecution and see if we can meet to discuss a possible compromise. I have a feeling their case could rest on the shoulders of this kid because there are a number of other unanswered questions we can expose. Unless the prosecuting attorney is an absolute fool, she's going to know this as well. However, before I reach out to her, there's something that's been really bothering me since we first got together, and this is where I need your feedback. Let me ask you a very important question, Edward, that I want you to carefully think about before you respond. You've finally gotten yourself into a position that many can only dream of. You're going to be financially secure for the rest of your life due to Ridgeley's generosity, assuming we win this case. Based on the short amount of time that we've been together, I'm convinced that nothing is more important to you than this new-found financial freedom that's currently within your grasp. Am I correct in this assumption?" Edward thought about the question imposed, and as he reflected back on his career and his life in general, he realized that Mize was spot-on in his assessment. Edward's life had always revolved around his personal obsession with money, including the lifestyle and security that went along with it. Ridgeley had set him up for life, and there was a part of this whole turn of events that Edward still struggled with. How in the world did all of this happen? Even though he and Ridgeley were always close, he was still amazed at the fact that Ridgeley left everything for him. Sylvia had every right to be livid over her absence in the trust, and Edward knew it. Deep down inside, this was what he struggled with the most...why was he the one chosen by Ridgeley? Edward could feel his mind begin to race, only to be interrupted by the shout that would soon come his way.

"Edward!" yelled Mize. "Did you hear my question? Do you want to be rich and free...or do you want to go to prison for the rest of your life?" Edward looked over at Mize and, for a brief moment in time, he could feel his blood begin to boil. "Mize, first of all, quit worrying about the boy," replied Edward. "I don't think the kid even knows how to talk, and he certainly isn't going to help us in this case. Worrying about him is just a waste of time for us. And as far as the question you're asking me now, you know what I want. I'm not even going to waste my time with an answer." Mize glared back at

Edward and for a split second, he felt like reaching over and snapping him like a twig...but for now, he would somehow find a way to maintain his composure. Patience was not one of Mize's strongest points, but he really didn't have a choice right now. Acting out of instinct rather than intellect would only hurt his ultimate objective, which was something he simply could not afford to have happen.

Abby made her way to her cluttered office and shut the door behind her. She reached out for the ringing phone on the corner of her desk, hoping this was the call she had been waiting for. Boxes were still unpacked due to the fact that she was relatively new to the job, not to mention that the Conners case had completely consumed her life since it first landed on her desk. How nice it would have been, she thought, to have had a couple of months to get acclimated to her new position before the biggest case the county had ever seen came her way...but this was not the case. "Hello, this is Abby Holt. How can I help you?" asked Abby, as she waited for the voice on the other end of the line. "Ms. Holt, this is Warren Mize. I'm sure you know who I am. First of all, let me congratulate you on your new position. Certainly, you had no idea you were signing up for the Conners mess when you took the job, so I'm hoping we can get this over with quickly. After all, it's obvious to everyone involved that Mr. Conners is guilty of nothing. He was simply in the wrong place at the wrong time. How would you like to get together for a drink so we can discuss how best to resolve this case...before you get thrown into a situation you're not prepared for?" Abby thought for a moment and sat down to catch her breath. "Mr. Mize, first of all, let me thank you for your kind words. Coming from a man as famous as you, your words truly mean a lot to me. Having said that, I need you to know that I'm not interested in any plea bargain. Your client is in big trouble, and we both know it. My responsibility is to make sure he never has the opportunity to do this again. His negligence cost Olivia Sanders her life, and now her only son is an orphan. How am I supposed to explain to little Benjamin why the only person in his life, the only reason for his existence, is now gone? I appreciate your well wishes and your offer to settle, but you can't be serious, Mr. Mize, now can you? Oh, and one other thing, Mr. Mize. . . if you have any thought of meeting with Benjamin before the trial, you can forget about it. He will not be seeing anyone at this time. Now, I need to get on with my day. I'm truly looking forward to our time together in the courtroom. See you soon." Mize heard the click of the phone echo in his ear, as his face turned flush red with the anger that had been building up for quite some time. Slowly, he made his way to the window and gazed out at the buildings below. In due time, he would crush this girl, and anyone else who stood in his way. It was only a matter of time...

Celeste slowly made her way out of the kitchen and into the darkened living room. Settling into her chair, she took out the calendar from her purse and began to look at the circled dates in front of her. Soon, she would be paying another visit to her most important client, Mr. Edward Conners, and she needed to be ready for the sequence of events that would be coming her way. Since her last visit to his cell, there were a number of things that were falling into place. However, Celeste also knew that her future would depend on an error free implementation of the plan that was in her hands now. Anything less than a perfect outcome would have a direct impact on everyone involved, most notably herself. Visits to the committee that watched her every move were infrequent; however, she knew they would be expecting nothing but good news on her next update. The trial would be starting just prior to her next visit with Conners; therefore, the details of their meeting would need to be finalized well in advance of the actual start date. Celeste carefully reviewed the weeks ahead and thought through her next steps. This would be her most visible hour in the eyes of the committee, and she could feel her pulse almost skip a beat as she thought about the days ahead. There would be no turning back now...

Chapter Six

Opening Arguments

A bby looked over her notes and thought about the case that would soon divide the county she now called home. She was in a very difficult position because she knew it was her job to prove that Edward Conners was negligent in the death of Olivia Sanders…but for Abby, it was more than just the verdict regarding the importance of this case. Looking across the table at little Benjamin, she couldn't help but think about a younger version of herself when she stared into his blue eyes. Knowing all too well what it was like to lose her mother, her heart broke at the thought of the little boy growing up without a mother or a father. It had been almost six months since the accident, and not once had the little boy uttered even a single word. No matter how hard Abby tried to get him to open up, he just stared off into the distance. Abby's case was resting on the shoulders of a sad, little boy who may never come out of it, but this was almost irrelevant to her. As important as it was to win the case, she was much more concerned about mending his heart right now. Somehow, Abby needed to find a way to repair the damage that was done when he lost his mother, but she was running out of ways to connect with him. She had heard about Mize in the courtroom, and she knew he would take no prisoners when it came to the interrogation of Benjamin. Her case rested on what Benjamin may have seen, which meant her case was shaky at best. If only she could find a way to reach him, then maybe she could determine what really happened on that cold, dark night. One thing was for certain. Lives were now hanging in the balance, and Abby's life would soon be engulfed by the courtroom she had dreamed about since she was a young girl back in Idaho. From the time Abby was barely out of the crib, all she wanted to be was a lawyer. Now, she was about to live the dream...but nobody ever told her about little boys like Benjamin. There was no way she could have ever prepared for something like this...

Even though the trial was scheduled to start at 9:00 a.m., the courtroom began to fill well in advance of the opening statements. This was the case that had captured the curiosity of everyone in Epoch County, and Abby was on display for all to see. Abby could feel her heart begin to race, as she reached over and held on to Benjamin's little hands. "Benjamin, I know this is a scary time for you, but I promise I'm not going to let anyone harm you," said Abby, as she leaned over and whispered in his left ear. "I want you here with me in the courthouse today because I feel like it's important for the jurors to see you in person. This may be the last time you're asked to be here unless one of us calls you to answer a few questions. You're going to do just great. You will be sitting in the seat right behind me today, and you won't have to say anything. If you need anything at all during the day, just tap me on the shoulder and I'll help with whatever you need." Benjamin looked over at Abby and said nothing. Deep down inside, he didn't like the fact that he was going to be on display for everyone to see.

"Ladies and gentlemen of the jury," remarked Abby, as she faced the 12 individuals who would soon be determining the fate of Edward Conners. "My name is Abby Holt, and I am the District Attorney for Epoch County. My role at this trial is very simple. I am here to prosecute Mr. Edward Conners, to show that Edward Conners was directly responsible for the death of Olivia Sanders. We will show that Mr. Conners was in an act of rage when the crime was committed; an uncontrollable state of mind that erupted through a series of events that had taken place earlier in the day. This case is all about sending a strong message to everyone that this kind of irresponsible negligence cannot be tolerated at any level in society today because the negative impact can be irreparable. His close friend and largest client, Mr. Andrew Ridgeley III, died earlier that day. As soon as Mr. Conners found out about the death of his friend, he knew his life would never be the same again. You see, Mr. Conners had made a fortune over the years off his old friend, Mr. Ridgeley. He knew the lifestyle he had grown to love was in jeopardy now, and his primary source of revenue was gone. In fact, his premonition about a change in lifestyle was confirmed when he received a phone call from Mr. Ridgeley's wife, Sylvia, that same evening. Sylvia called Mr. Conners on his phone, and that's when his life was truly turned upside down. Mr. Conners received the news that he was fired, and then he received a second call regarding the elimination of his company car as well. This is what set him off just seconds before he plowed into Olivia Sanders's car that was parked on the side of the road. The force of the crash killed her, but miraculously, her little boy survived. As a result of Mr. Conners's irrational behavior and uncontrollable anger, this little boy seated right here in the second row of this courthouse is now alone... without his mother! All of this could have been avoided if Edward Conners had been able to control his temper. I will show, without a doubt, that this selfish act cost Olivia Sanders her life...and now her son, Benjamin, is forced to live the rest of his life remembering the image of the crash that took his mother away forever." The courtroom came to a hush, as nearly all eyes were glued on the little boy with the blue eyes. Abby looked over at the jury and took a deep breath. She wasn't quite through yet. "Ladies and gentlemen of the jury, this case is much more important than the terminology you will be hearing throughout the trial. Words like negligence, selfishness, irrational, and uncontrollable can best be described by staring into the eyes of a child...and in this case, that child is sitting right here, and his name is Benjamin Sanders." Abby made her way back to her seat and could feel Mize's glaring eyes cut through her like a knife. Game on, Abby thought, as she settled back into her seat...

Mize slowly made his way up to the jury box and said nothing. He looked into the eyes of every member, and then he smiled. Somehow, he needed to get this team of 12 back on his side. Mize needed them to get the image of the boy out of their mind as quickly as possible, and he knew it wouldn't be easy. "Ladies and gentlemen of the jury," said Mize, as he smiled into the eyes of the jurors who would ultimately determine the fate of his client. "My name is Warren Mize, and I represent Mr. Edward Conners. It's a tremendous privilege to be with you today, and I greatly appreciate the service you are exemplifying by being here in this courtroom. I realize that all of you have very busy schedules so having you fulfill your civic duties by sitting on this jury is not going unnoticed by myself and the rest of my defense team. I do think it is important for us to take a very close look at the case you're about to hear starting today. Let me preface my opening statements by saying that I'm quite frankly surprised we're even here today, given the facts of the case. I have more experience in this courtroom than anyone else in Epoch County, and I have to be honest with you. When I was first asked about taking on this case, I scratched my head to see if there was something I was missing. You see...I've tried numerous cases fairly similar to this one in the past, and I just couldn't understand what all the scuttlebutt was about. I mean, why in the world was so much attention being paid to a case that was nothing more than an unfortunate situation brought on by Ms. Sanders? Then, it dawned on me. It had to be about the money. Edward Conners is being targeted because he has money, not because he did anything wrong, but because he represents something that the prosecuting attorney wants a piece of. This case is all about her career; it's about making a case out of something that should have been thrown out long before it ever got into this court of law. It has become obvious to all that this case is nothing more than a waste of taxpayers' monies, which by the way means it impacts each and every one of us in the courtroom today. Indirectly, all of us are paying for this charade...all because the prosecuting attorney wants to make a name for herself. Edward Conners did nothing wrong. Every single one of us in this courtroom today feels awful for little Benjamin Sanders. But...we need to be careful about falling into the trap of making a decision based on sympathy rather than the facts of the case. Ms. Holt would love for us to focus our attention on little Benjamin. Why else would she parade him into this courtroom to gain your sympathy vote, so to speak? The whole thing makes me sick. Instead of focusing our attention on Benjamin, we really should be focused on my client and what he is up against here in this case. I would ask that you put yourself in his shoes and think about how you'd feel if you were dragged into this courtroom after doing nothing wrong. After decades of representing Andrew Ridgeley, he was fired on the same day as the loss of one of his closest friends. Sure...he was angry, but I need to emphasize that he was in a lot of pain due to the personal loss he had suffered. Our case will show, without a shadow of doubt, that Olivia Sanders's car was not parked correctly on the side of the road. In fact, her car was out in the lane of traffic, which is what caused Edward Conners to veer off and hit it on the night in question. Why she was parked out in the middle of traffic, we will never know. We all feel terrible for young Benjamin because of his loss, but the bottom line is Olivia Sanders was killed because of her negligence, not my client's. She should have had her car parked on the side of the road with her flashers on…but she had neither. And, this is what killed her! We will show that Edward Conners, in fact, did nothing wrong. He is being tried because he happens to have a large bank account, but it doesn't mean that his name should be dragged through the mud over the coming weeks. I have looked at the background of this jury, and I must say it is one of the most impressive juries I have ever had the opportunity to work with. I also know that many of you have been highly successful in your respective careers. I would hate to think that any of you could ever be in the same position as my client, Edward Conners, is today…not because of what you may have done, but instead, because you represent success in your own life. Please, keep this in mind as we move forward. Put yourself in the shoes of my client. Think about how scared you would be if your life had been torn apart because of something you had no control over. This is the position of my client here today. Edward Conners has become the victim because we have a prosecuting attorney who is on a mission to elevate her career, regardless of who goes down in the process. She doesn't care about doing the right thing. As I stated before, she simply cares only about winning, as evidenced by her willingness to use the face of a little boy to tug at the heartstrings of the courtroom here today. Quite frankly, I am sickened to my stomach that she has the audacity to show up and parade an innocent child in front of you in order to gain sympathy at his expense... merely for her benefit. Thankfully, we have assembled one of the most intelligent team of jurors that I have ever been associated with in my 30 years as a lawyer. Once again, thank you for taking time out of your busy lives to be here with us today. I have no doubt in my mind that your intelligence has been insulted by our new district attorney, Ms. Holt. My promise to you is that I will never allow this to happen with anyone who sits on my defense team. I look forward to working with you to make sure we do the right thing together. Experience tells me that you as a jury are different, and that you have been underestimated by the opposition over here regarding your personal intelligence, wisdom, and overall affinity for doing the right thing. I will not feed into this ignorance. I am grateful to be here for you...and to protect you, if need be."

Edward watched in awe, as Mize made his way back to his seat. In all his years as an attorney, never before had Edward ever witnessed such a powerful opening statement. In a matter of minutes, Mize had successfully shifted the focus of the jury from the little boy with the blue eyes over to the perceived ego of the new district attorney, Abby Holt. Since none of the jurors had ever met Abby and knew nothing about her background, Mize's strategy was brilliant.

From his perspective, this case was not about a little boy who had his mother taken away, but instead was the byproduct of an aggressive, young attorney whose sole focus was on the growth of her own career. He had successfully painted Abby as an outsider who blew into town and insulted the valued members of the community. Mize looked over at Edward and nodded his head because he could sense that he immediately had the jury right where he wanted them. Mize was the best, and he knew it. In an instant, Edward's confidence began to soar, and he felt an inexplicable connection to Mize. He was different than any other man Edward had ever come in contact with, as his personality had a way of consuming its target. Edward focused on the jury and could see their heads nodding in agreement, while Mize settled back into his chair. Mize had connected with every face in the box, and now it was just a matter of time before he would move in for the kill. Edward looked over at the prosecution and felt an immediate sense of confidence consume his body. Abby's face turned flush because she knew Mize's immediate partnership with the courtroom was real. She could feel her mind race back to law school to one of the very first lectures she attended shortly after enrollment. "Most cases are either won or lost at the beginning or end of the trial," said the infamous Professor Highler, Associate Dean of Law. "The middle of the trial should be the focal point for the members of the jury but, in most cases, it is not. Bottom line…don't ever get beat in your opening statement or your closing remarks, or your chances of winning will be slim. While the body of work as an attorney in the court of law is critical, nothing can ever replace a powerful start or finish to a trial. Most jury members have the attention span of a gnat; they remember the beginning and the end...and not much more." Abby felt a lump in her throat begin to develop, as she assessed her performance since the opening bell. She knew the first round went to Mize, and now her reputation was at stake. Nobody could have ever prepared her for this at law school...

"Edward, let's stop and get a drink," said Mize, as he and Edward made their way out of the courtroom at the end of day one. "There's something I want to talk with you about, totally unrelated to our case." "Sure thing, Warren," responded Edward, as he made his way out to the limousine that was waiting in front. By the tone of Mize's voice, Edward could sense that this meeting was going to be different than others conducted up to this point. "Thomas, take us down to The Club on the edge of town and wait for us out back. Edward and I are going to get a drink and a bite to eat. Call Maury before we get there so we can get one of the tables in back. I need to have some privacy with my client." Thomas reached for the phone and made the call. Mize and Edward sat down in the back of the limo, both exhausted from a long and successful day one. Mize closed his eyes, while Edward waited for a question or statement to come his way. Instead, silence filled the back seat, as both men could feel the early momentum of the trial quickly moving over to their camp. Thomas turned into the darkened alley and parked the car around back. Edward followed Mize through the back door, while they quickly made their way to the open booth in the corner of the restaurant. Mize reached up and closed the curtain behind them, with Edward close behind. Mize had been waiting for this conversation to take place for quite some time and could sense that tonight, the timing was absolutely perfect.

On the other side of town, Abby stared at her laptop, while she replayed the events of the day. Darkness had settled in, as she began to think back on how her case had gotten off to such a shaky start. Deep down inside, she knew she had underestimated Mize and his ability to move a jury his way. The scouting report on him said he was one of the best in the area, but she never expected such a quick turn of events. Mize was right about one thing. Abby's attempt at getting the jury to focus their attention on Benjamin had backfired, and now she would be scrambling for equal billing once again. The case was just getting started, and she already had two strikes against her...she simply could not afford a third. Abby could still see the look in Benjamin's eyes, as they left the court-room at the end of the day. The little boy didn't have to say a word because his eyes did all the talking. After bringing him into the courtroom that morning, Abby wasn't sure if he would ever trust her again. Mize's words earlier in the day had a huge impact on everyone attending, but nobody was impacted more than Benjamin. Abby had to find a way to explain her position to him, or she may never get him back. Her case was already shaky at best, and without Benjamin, she knew her chances of winning would be slim at best.

"Edward, first of all, today was a terrific start for us," said Mize, as he leaned back in his chair. "Our strategy totally caught the prosecution off guard, and now we have little Ms. Holt on the run. Although it would be very easy for us to rest on our laurels, we need to bury her and this silly case as quickly as possible. I want to turn up the heat on her and watch her squirm. Once we break her down, I'll ask her to throw out the case based on lack of evidence. I have no intention to call the kid to the stand because this will only risk our position of strength right now. Plus, he seems like he has some kind of problem. I can't tell if it's autism or a neurological condition, but the kid doesn't seem like he's normal to me. I really don't think he can help us so we'll move forward without him. The last thing we need is to have him get up there and play on the hearts of the jurors. But...let's get on with the real reason we're meeting tonight. Edward, I've been observing you for the past couple of months, and I must say that I'm very impressed with your ability to focus on the job at hand. I've deliberately come at you with the intent to rile you up, yet you've been able to maintain your composure with every test. What I'm about to tell you is something that cannot leave this table. By sharing this information with you, I am trusting you with something that needs to stay between you and me. Do you understand what I'm saying, Edward? This is very, very important."

Edward pulled his chair closer to Mize and leaned forward. "Warren, you have my word," replied Edward. "Nothing we discuss here tonight will ever go any further."

Mize smiled, leaned forward, and began to speak just a few decibels louder than a whisper. "Edward, I've come across a deal that I haven't shared with anyone yet. Quite honestly, I've been looking for another partner who has the same will to win as myself, and I'm convinced that I've found my man in you. Edward, I'd like to bring you into the loop regarding a once-in-a-lifetime opportunity. There's a small start-up company that has just developed a new technology. In a nutshell, it could be one of the most important developments from a technological standpoint that the world has ever seen. Without going into a lot of detail, the company has developed a microchip that can be modified to address many of the most common cognitive disorders and handicaps in the world today. In some of the most prevalent disease states, this chip has the ability to identify the specific marker that is causing the deficiency to occur. For instance, the chip can be embedded into the brain and through sensory adaptation; it can identify those markers that are responsible for patients who are blind, deaf, and dumb. Edward, can you imagine the impact this company will have if we are able to patent this technology and market it around the world? Every major laboratory and hospital in the world will want a piece of the action because without the capability of doing these procedures, their loss of revenue due to insufficient technology will be enormous. There are over 170 million people in the world today who fall into one of these three categories. The impact of this technology will be unlike anything we've ever seen before. I have a team of investors in place, and I need one more individual to round out our executive board of seven. You're the last piece to the puzzle, Edward. Is this something you'd be interested in pursuing as soon as we end the trial?"

Edward thought for a moment and nodded his head in agreement. "Wow, that sounds incredible, Warren. Absolutely, I'm interested." responded Edward. "When do you plan to move forward, and what are you looking for from me?" "Edward, first of all, my investors have already given me full clearance to bring you into the circle, assuming you want to be part of the team. I told them all about you, and they're comfortable with my recommendation to add you to our executive board of directors. I can tell you that each of them is a major player in the area. The individuals on the team obviously need to maintain anonymity because their positions in the community are highly visible. They don't want anyone to know that they're working together on a project that hasn't even gone public yet. I thought about waiting to share this information with you, but clinical trials are scheduled for early next month. Funding needs to be in place before we can actually move forward with Phase 1. We're estimating that our research and development costs for the project are going to total just under $70M, which means that each of us will have an equal share in the company for individual contributions of $10M. I realize that Ridgeley's portfolio left for you was worth close to $10M, so this may be an investment that works well into your plans. I have the papers in my briefcase, and I want you to look them over this weekend. If this is something you want to be part of, then I'm going to need your signature first thing on Monday. Make sure you don't tell anyone about this for a couple of reasons. First of all, the implementation of this project is going to be done with a very small team in place. We're doing this because we can't afford for this information to get out into the market. We plan on doing an IPO as soon as we clear Phase 1, and this needs to be done after our patent is secure. We simply cannot afford for any competitors to catch wind of this project, or it will cost us millions. First to market with any technology is key; therefore, we need to make sure this position of power is not at risk. Edward, we're bringing you on because we trust you. This is the last time we'll discuss this agreement because we don't want it to get in the way of your trial. Once your trial is over and you're acquitted, then we can move on with the implementation of our plan. You've seen me work my magic in the courtroom, and I fully intend to have this case wrapped up in the next month or so. There is absolutely no way we'll lose this case. You're going to see this same performance from me when you and I are business partners. Our new company is going to literally change the way this world diagnoses and treats patients. Nothing in the history of the medical field has ever come close to what we have in our hands right now. As soon as the trial ends, then we move on this business deal. Our $70M investment should be converted over to $1B in no time, which means that each of the primary investors, including yourself, will be looking at a personal split of over $125M each. Edward, I've been around a long time and I've never seen anything like this. This truly is an opportunity that only comes around once in a lifetime." Edward looked over at Mize and felt a smile come over his face, as he thought about what Mize had just told him. One thing was for certain…a man could do a whole lot with $125M.

Chapter Seven

The Second Wish

E dward lay in bed and felt his body relax for the first time in over a month. The trial had gotten off to an incredible start, and Edward could sense that everything was finally going his way. Mize was even better than he had expected, and Edward was certain the case would be wrapped up in less than a month. He sat up, took a deep breath, and slowly made his way out of the bedroom and into the hallway. Rubbing the sleep from his eyes, Edward opened the front door and walked down the sidewalk to get the morning newspaper. Finally, a day to myself, Edward thought, as he reached down to pick up the dew-soaked rag that had been part of his life for years. As he made his way back toward the porch, Edward noticed an envelope attached to his mailbox. No postmark on the outside of the card meant that whoever delivered the letter must have done so in person. Edward shook his head and closed the door behind him. Suddenly, the card in the mailbox carried a much higher priority than the newspaper, and Edward sat down to read its message...

Dear Mr. Conners:

It has been six months since my last visit to see you. Hopefully, you haven't forgotten the deal I presented to you while you were incarcerated after your accident. Your first wish was granted, and now we are ready to move forward with your second one. I need to meet with you this evening in Old Town. I will be at the old shed behind mile marker 113. You need to come by at 7:00 p.m. sharp with your decision regarding your second wish. I don't anticipate our meeting taking more than five minutes, assuming you are ready to tell me your plan. Just like the first wish, it will go into effect first thing tomorrow morning.

Bye for now...
Celeste

Edward stared down at the envelope and thought about the note that had been left for him. How in the world could this "wish thing" be possible...this was one of the craziest things he had ever seen! When he communicated his first wish to the old woman in his cell, he was in a totally different frame of mind than he was in right now. There was no way he could possibly think that an old lady who visited him in prison was somehow responsible for the implementation of his first wish. But then again, Edward realized deep down inside that his appointment as the sole beneficiary of the Ridgeley estate made no sense at all. Certainly, he wasn't voicing this skepticism out loud, but Edward knew there was no logical explanation whatsoever for the recent sequence of events. As Edward looked back at the past six months since the implementation of his first wish, his life was definitely moving in the right direction. Financially, he was in a position that he never thought possible...and now Mize wanted him to be a partner for a company on the cutting edge of changing the world. As much as Edward wanted to dispute the logic behind the three wishes, he wasn't about to test the waters now...not after the first wish had turned out to be nothing short of a miracle. He sat down at the kitchen table and started to think about the meeting that was less than 12 hours away. Edward could feel himself start to laugh, as he began to contemplate his second wish. This would be an easy one. His mind drifted back to his first wish, which turned out to be even better than he could have ever imagined. Ridgeley's estate had been served up to Edward on a silver platter, and now here he was with an opportunity to multiply those numbers tenfold! Even though the old woman gave him the creeps, it was hard to argue with the results. He had no idea who she was, but right now, he could care less. She was the ticket to his newfound wealth, and he wasn't about to question who she was or where in the world she came from. Edward could almost feel his body feed off the greed that had consumed him, which was even more prevalent than before the night of the accident. The more Edward was able to accumulate, the more he wanted. He loved the lifestyle that money could bring, and now he was ready to take his desire to the next level. Although he was in the midst of a trial that literally held his life in check, he had no concern whatsoever. Mize was in control, and Edward was merely along for the ride. As much as Edward hated Mize at the beginning of their relationship, his admiration for the man who controlled his future had grown to a whole new level over the past couple weeks. He had the utmost confidence in Mize's ability to take him to places he only dreamed of in the past. Edward threw the envelope on the table and reached for the newspaper. His second wish was a no-brainer, and now it was time to relax. After all, Edward had a very big day ahead of him.

Abby reached for the phone and began to dial the number of her very best friend in the world because he always seemed to say the right thing. Since she was first promoted to district attorney, Abby found herself shying away from these discussions because she wanted to tackle the world alone. However, today she felt much different. She was losing her first big case, but worst of all, Mize was humiliating her in the process. She needed to speak with the one who had been there since she was a little girl...the one who made it clear to her that he would never leave her. She dialed the number from memory and immediately felt a peace take hold of her body. "Hello, this is William Holt," said the voice, while Abby waited for her chance to respond. "Daddy," responded Abby, "I hope I'm not bothering you tonight. I've been missing you a lot, so I thought I'd give you a call." "Oh, honey," replied William. "It's so good to hear your voice. I've been missing you a lot lately. What's on your mind tonight, sweetheart? Is everything ok?" Abby could feel her voice start to quiver, as she thought about how she could honestly answer the question, yet keep her father from worrying in the process. Nobody knew her better than her dad, so sugarcoating her answer just wasn't going to work. "I'm doing all right, daddy, but I'm hoping you can give me some advice. As you know, I can't go into any specific details about the case I'm heading up out here right now, but I'm feeling a little outmatched in the courtroom. I'm up against one of the strongest attorneys in the country who relishes the opportunity to rub my face in the dirt whenever he can. I was just wondering if this ever happened to you when you were younger, and if it did, what did you do about it? I could really use your help here. I'm having a very difficult time getting back on my feet again, and you know this just isn't like me." William knew it took a lot for his little girl to call him for advice. Since the accident took place nearly three decades earlier, William and Abby had literally become one. He was always available to share his words of encouragement with her, and Abby was always there to show her father just how much she loved him. Since she left Idaho for law school and then on to her career on the East Coast, William just didn't get to see her near as much as he would have liked. This call came at a perfect time for both of them, as he settled into his den. Hopefully, he would have the right words to say that would help ease her pain. After all, Abby was still his little girl...and, by the sound of her voice, it was obvious to William that she was hurting real bad right now.

Edward gathered his thoughts and made his way around the dark corner toward mile marker 113. It would have been a whole lot easier, he thought, if there were additional street lights on such a dark night. This was one section of town that Edward never frequented, and for good reason. Edward continued to walk toward the white marker barely sticking out of the ground, hoping that this was, in fact, mile marker 113. Pulling the grass back from the side of the stake, Edward slowly made his way to the numbers. He felt a momentary sigh of relief when the number 113 was revealed. Off to his right, Edward could see the old shed that was referenced in the note. Who in the world would ever be down here on a night like this, Edward thought, as he planned his next move. Slowly, Edward began to move closer to the shed and could see a dim, yellow light near the room in the back. Stepping up on the darkened porch, he proceeded to move through the front door and on toward the back of the rat-infested structure. Edward could hear the pattering of little feet run on ahead of him, as they seemed to pave the way for him to make it to the room with the light. "Come in and have a seat, Mr. Conners," whispered the voice from the darkness. "I've been waiting for you."

"Abby, let me tell you about a situation I ran into early on in my career. Based on what you're telling me, it may have significant relevance regarding what you're up against right now. My first position in management was one of my most difficult. I had been asked to take on the worst performing operation in the country, and I was expected to make rapid changes that would turn things around fast. When I first arrived at our distribution center, there was an older man waiting for me. He made it very clear to me right from the start that he wasn't happy I got the job because he believed he was more qualified and deserving of the position. Quite honestly, he may have been right. I had only been with the company for three years, and he had been with the organization for almost 20. Anyway, the guy was out to get me from day one. I didn't trust him at all, and I knew he would go to any lengths to get me fired. One day, my boss called me into the office and told me that the internal auditors found a huge discrepancy in our numbers. There had been a shortage of nearly $5,000 from the week before, and he wanted to know if I knew anything about it. In one breath, he was asking me to help him identify the thief; while in the other, he was insinuating that I may be the one responsible for the loss. I had no doubt in my mind that Walt Jones, the guy who wanted my job because he was bypassed during the interview process, was the one who took the money. I brought every employee into my office and asked all of them a series of questions, but every single employee denied any wrongdoing. Finally, my boss became extremely agitated with the entire situation and he told me that if I didn't find the perpetrator myself within the next week, that he would get rid of me and do it himself. On my last day of that week, I knew my hours were numbered. Then, at about 2:00 that afternoon, I went into the top drawer of my desk and found a note that had been placed there while I was at a meeting after lunch. In bold letters, the note read "CHECK WALT'S LUNCHBOX". So, that is what I did. I proceeded to take my assistant with me into the cubicle where Jones worked, and I reached around the side of his desk. I opened the lunchbox, and in his thermos, were five one-hundred dollar bills. We called in our internal auditor and ran the numbers. We were exactly five hundred dollars short that day. On my way back to my office, I thanked my assistant for the tip she gave me regarding the money in Jones's office. She told me she had no idea what I was talking about, and I was totally perplexed as to who had tipped me off. Then, five years later, I received a letter from a man who worked in our building. He was our maintenance man and, quite frankly, nobody ever noticed the guy and very few people ever said anything to him. I just happened to be one of the few managers who was nice to him, and I guess he decided to pay me back. In the letter, he told me that he was the one who tipped me off about Jones. He also told me that the reason he never shared this with me when it happened five years earlier was quite simple…it was because I never asked. All I had to do was ask him, and he would have told me everything. The reason I'm telling you this story, honey, is that this experience taught me a valuable lesson. It taught me that sometimes our greatest findings happen in the area that we least expect it. Some of the most important answers aren't found at the executive level of an organization. Good managers, and lawyers I presume as well, are very good at peeling back the "layers of the onion" that others neglect. When I went through my experience with Walt Jones and the missing money, I expended all of my energy on battling him. I was out to prove that I was the boss, and the decision in hiring me was the right one. This kept me from uncovering the truth. . . the truth that disguised itself as the maintenance man who cleaned my office floor every night. My only advice to you, sweetheart, is don't let this seasoned lawyer distract you. All it will do is separate you from the real answers you need. Close your eyes and turn to God for His guidance. I believe with all my heart that He will give you the strength you need to fight through this temporary setback, and in the end, you will be much stronger for it." Abby gathered her thoughts and didn't know what to say. Her father was right on target with his assessment of her situation. Silence continued to capture the airwaves, as Abby thought about how her father's experience from years gone by had relevance in her life today. Finally, Abby gathered up her strength and said, "Thank you, Daddy. You're absolutely right. I know exactly what I need to do now. I love you." "I love you too, honey," replied William. "Please, call anytime. I'm always here if you need me." As William hung up the phone, he thought back to the years that had come and gone in the blink of an eye. His Abby was all grown up now, but to William, she would always be his little girl.

Edward ducked his head under the door frame that led to the room with the light. In the same motion, he brushed away the cobwebs that lined the wooden structure and made his way to the chair waiting for him just inside the entrance. The voice was coming from the corner of the room; however, Edward still couldn't see the outline of the face that was obviously waiting for his answer. "Mr. Conners, thank you for being on time here tonight," said Celeste, while she kept her face hidden in the dark confines of the old, wooden shed. "This discussion shouldn't take long at all. By now, you know the rules of this game. I need you to tell me what your second wish will be, and similar to the first, your decision will go into effect starting tomorrow. This will leave you with one last wish, which will be granted exactly six months from this evening. I assume you've been thinking about how you'd like to proceed, so let's not waste any time. Mr. Conners, what would you like your second wish to be?" Edward looked over at the darkened corner and thought about his answer. Oh, how he wanted to uncover the physical identity of the voice that came his way. On the other hand, there was a part of him that just wanted to make his wish and get the heck out of there. "Celeste, my second wish is an easy one," responded Edward. "I've been presented with the opportunity of a lifetime. I can't get into any details here this evening; however, I'd be a fool to let this offer pass me by. My second wish is that my investment in the partnership that I've been offered brings me unsurpassed wealth. As a result, I will experience a newfound status in this community…one that I've only dreamed about in the past."

Celeste looked over at Edward and paused for a moment. Slowly, she motioned her hands forward and said, "Your wish will be granted, Mr. Conners. Now, go get on with your evening. You and I will be meeting one more time in six months, and that will be the last of your three wishes. Until then, I wish you the best." Edward nodded his head and made his way to the door. Never before had the evening air felt so good, as he walked quickly to his car at the end of the street. As he drove away, Edward glanced back at the shed and saw Celeste's dark figure standing just inside the doorway. She watched as he made his way back on to the street that led him away from the shed. Edward reached over and hit the door locks, while he refocused his eyes on the road ahead. One last look and that would be it, Edward thought, as he turned his eyes back toward the shed behind him. Celeste's face was exposed for the very first time, and Edward could feel his heart begin to race. That look in her eyes was unlike anything he'd ever seen before…it was a look he hoped he would never see again.

Sweat dropped from Abby's forehead, as she reached over for the alarm clock that continued to torment her. The weekend had flown by at record pace, and now she would be expected to gather her senses and take on Mize once again. Lying in bed, she thought about the dream that routinely played tricks with her mind. The sequence of events leading up to the crash continued to haunt her, and she struggled with the question that just wouldn't go away. No matter how hard she tried, everything pointed to the little boy on the side of the road. Why wasn't he in the car with his mother when Conners's car slammed into it on the side of the road? It just didn't make any sense that he would be standing in front of their car all by himself. During his testimony, Conners repeatedly maintained the position that he was just standing there, but that didn't seem to add up at all. Because there were no witnesses, the jury was given no other option than to believe the testimony of Conners. No matter how hard Abby tried to focus on the other events of the night in question, her mind continually took her back to the issue that just wouldn't go away. Abby knew there was only one person who could answer the question that was the key to her case, but up until now, he hadn't said anything at all. Maybe it was time to pay another visit to the little boy, Abby thought, as she made her way to the bathroom. She may not have any other choice...

Edward leaned over to Mize, as the morning's participants began to enter the building. The weekend had gone by in a flash, and here they were once again in the courtroom that would ultimately determine Edward's fate. Mize leaned over as well and whispered into Edward's ear, "How was your weekend, Edward? Hopefully, you had the opportunity to think about our discussion. I assume you did, correct?" Keeping his head down, Edward turned back to Mize with his response and replied, "I'm in, Warren. Here you go." And with that, Mize had in his possession the signed papers he so dearly coveted. Mize could feel an immediate rush grab hold of him, as he calmly gave Edward a confident nod of approval. He opened his briefcase and slid Edward's envelope inside. Edward leaned back in his chair and began to think about the events of the day. Most of the pertinent witnesses had already been called to the bench, and nothing looked like it would stand in the way of his acquittal. Greed had settled into Edward's heart like a blood thirsty predator, while he thought about the new life that would soon be coming his way. Closing remarks would be shared with the jury that would ultimately decide Edward's outcome, and barring a catastrophic surprise, he would soon be home free. Finally, Edward would be in a position to enjoy the life he so desperately wanted...the one he had dreamed about ever since he was a young boy.

Chapter Eight

The Update

As the woman reached up to enter the code, she could feel her hand begin to shake at the thought of what waited for her on the other side of the door. Her update would hopefully be well-received, but the committee's response was always an unknown. Making her way through the door, Celeste had become accustomed to the room on the other side of the curtain. Voices came to a halt, while she made her way through the entrance. All eyes were upon her, as she sat down in the chair at the center of the room. She was never permitted to speak first, and through years of discipline, Celeste waited for her queue to answer the questions that would undoubtedly be coming her way. She kept her head down in fear of seeing something that would only come back to haunt her. Darkness engulfed the room, except for the dim light that came from just inside the door. Although it was hard for Celeste to determine the number of participants in the room on this particular night, she had a feeling from past experience that there were at least six. Similar to any of the previous committee meetings she attended in the past, the identity of every participant was always held under wraps. However, there was absolutely no doubt in anyone's mind as to who was running the show. "The time has come for you to provide us with a brief update," said the raspy voice from the front of the room. "I assume you are prepared to review the case of Edward Conners, is that correct?" Celeste felt her heart begin to race, as she slowly lifted her head. "Yes, sir, I am prepared. I met with Edward Conners this past weekend. As you know, it was time for him to make his second wish. Without going into all the details, he made it clear to me that he had been presented with an investment opportunity that he'd been waiting for his entire life. His wish was that this particular investment brought him unsurpassed wealth and prestige. I told him he could expect his second wish to go into effect the following day." Celeste had learned from year's past that her answers needed to be brief and to the point. The committee wasn't looking for personal narrative, only the facts. They would either be satisfied with her feedback…or she would be dead. There was no in-between. "Good work," replied the voice. "Conners has turned out to be no different than any of our targets from the past. He is naïve and gullible, which is good for us. At the end of the day, personal greed is the desire of all. Just like all the rest, his obsession with always having more will be his downfall as well. You may go now. We will be in touch with you once everything is finalized." Celeste stood up and slowly made her way out the door. She had survived another meeting and could only hope she would soon be home free. This assignment was much different than others in the past because the potential payoff, and the risk involved, was huge...

Richard Fletcher paced the room and reached for another cigarette. Hopefully, this would be the night that he would get his final instructions, and he could move forward with the plan. He would be the final piece of the puzzle, and all involved in the deadly trap knew that no other role would be more important than his. He rubbed the back of his neck, as the stress of what was about to happen felt like it was going to suffocate him. Fletcher took a deep breath and tried to relax, but it was impossible. Far too much was at stake, and lives would be changed based on the outcome of what was yet to come. Suddenly, the phone next to his bed rang, and Fletcher put the receiver to his ear. "Hello, this is Richard," answered Fletcher, hoping for the final instructions that would put the wheels in motion. "Fletcher, listen to me closely," said the voice on the other end of the line. "Everything is in place. You need to make your move in the next couple days and find a way to move that jury. I don't need to tell you that everything we've discussed is at stake. There is absolutely no room for error, Fletcher. You know what needs to be done." "Yes, sir. Everything we've talked about will soon go into effect," answered Fletcher. "Don't disappoint me, Fletcher," said the voice. "I will be watching this outcome very closely. An acquittal will cost you your life." And with that, Fletcher's ear was met with a dial tone. He put out his cigarette in the ashtray next to his bed and reached for the light. Slowly, he pulled the covers back and made his way into the bed that awaited him, staring at the ceiling fan that methodically spun above his tired and weathered face. Fletcher could feel the sweat begin to form on his forehead, as he thought about the week that was in front of him. His upcoming actions would have an impact on a number of individuals, and he knew the final outcome of their plan would be dependent on him. Hopefully, he would soon fall asleep and his conscience would take a much-needed reprieve. No matter how disgusted he was in himself, there was no backing out now...not if he wanted to live.

Monday turned out to be an uneventful day in the courtroom, as Mize and Abby traded jabs throughout the day. The two had developed a genuine disdain for one another, and the wounds were still fresh from their opening statements. Abby could feel her case slipping through her fingertips, while she continued to reach for answers that would help in her search for the truth. No matter how hard she tried, she still found it difficult to connect with little Benjamin. Bringing him back into the courtroom hadn't happened since the first day of the trial because Abby didn't want to put him through any additional trauma after the loss of his mother. Benjamin had become a ward of the state after the accident, and now he was simply waiting for the system to assign him to their customary foster parents of choice. Similar to other kids in the same predicament, Benjamin's ability to influence his next step in this convoluted process would be minimal at best. In the interim, he would simply wait for a family to step forward. On this particular night, Abby decided to stop by one last time and try to see if the two of them could find some common ground. If only Abby could reach out and comfort him in some way, she would do so in a heartbeat. Benjamin had been through a lot, and he would soon be starting over once again. Closing arguments for the case were scheduled for the end of the week, and Abby knew there was a strong possibility that Conners would soon walk. If only she could find a way to bring Benjamin back to the night that changed everything...

Abby pulled up in front of the old, brick building and could feel her heart drop to the floor. To think that one event in Benjamin's life could take him from the confines of his safe, little home to a place like this made Abby sick to her stomach. She reached around to the back seat of her car and grabbed the gift bag with the bright blue wrapping paper. Hopefully, there would be something inside the bag that would help bring a smile to Benjamin's face. It had been a very long time since he had a reason to smile, but maybe tonight would be different. "Hello, Ms. Holt. How are you this evening?" asked the receptionist at the front desk. "Who are you here to visit tonight?" "How are you doing, Linda?" replied Abby. "I'm here to see Benjamin Sanders. He's not expecting me, but I'm hoping that's a good thing. I didn't want him to go into a shell because I'm here. If you could let the ladies up on the 4th Floor know I'm here, that would be great." "I understand, ma'am. I'll let them know," responded Linda, as she reached for the phone. Abby made her way to the seating area and waited for the directive to head on up to see Benjamin. Holding on to the package that accompanied her made Abby feel like she had a purpose...hopefully, Benjamin would feel the same way. Tonight, Abby's objective was clear. She could only hope and pray that the outcome would be a good one as well. She was here to make Benjamin smile; to somehow convert his sadness over to the joy that had eluded him since the night he lost his mother. Somehow...she had to rebuild his trust in her once again.

"Edward, tonight will be the last night we're together away from the courtroom until after the trial," said Mize, while he reached for the chilled bottle of red wine. "Martelli's is one of my favorite restaurants, so I thought it was only fitting that we meet here tonight for our last dinner before the final verdict is reached. Our closing arguments should be coming up in a couple of days, and then the case will be going to the jury. I want you to know that I've deposited your $10M investment into our corporate account because I wanted to make sure everything was in place before the trial ended. The signed papers you gave me on Monday are now in our safety deposit box in order to ensure absolute anonymity regarding our partnership. As soon as you are acquitted, we will convert your investment over to preliminary shares of stock in our new company. This is consistent with the other members of our executive team. Once we finalize our Initial Public Offering, your stock price will obviously go up based on the reaction of the market. Edward, you can expect to at least quadruple your investment during this first 90 days of the IPO. I want to wait until after the trial to move on the communication of our new company to potential investors, just to alleviate any questions that may come our way. We can't afford to raise any suspicions at this juncture, so you'll want to make sure you don't say anything to anybody." "Warren, I understand," replied Edward. "However, I do expect to be very involved in the strategic direction of our new company. As soon as the dust settles after the acquittal, I expect to help lead our team. I want to play a major role in everything we do." Mize looked over at Edward and leaned forward, while he gestured for Edward to move closer. "I would expect nothing less from you, Edward," replied Mize. "You can trust me."

Abby rode the elevator on up to the 4th Floor and waited for the doors to open. For whatever reason, tonight felt different than others in the past, and she could only hope that the outcome would be positive as well. She made her way closer and closer to Benjamin's room at the end of the hallway and could feel a lump begin to develop in her throat. Abby's nerves were working overtime, while she thought about his sad face waiting for her on the other side of the door. What in the world could she possibly say to the little boy that would bring him the peace he needed after the loss he had suffered? Since the night of the accident, Abby did all she could to stay away from this facility because it brought back all the memories of her own loss decades ago. It was impossible for Abby not to think about what may have happened had her dad not survived the crash that took her mother and little sister. More than likely, Abby would have ended up just like

Benjamin, waiting for a replacement to the only family she ever knew. Abby closed her eyes and prayed for the words that would somehow bring comfort to her newfound, little friend. Oh, how she wanted to make Benjamin's life a little bit better...even if it was just for one night.

Entering the room, Abby soon made her way over to where Benjamin was resting. The staff indicated to her that Benjamin very seldom left the confines of his room and, more often than not, spent most of his time in bed resting. He had been through a lot; however, Abby knew firsthand that it was important for him to find a way to move on. Lying around would only bring him back to the way life used to be, and Abby knew this was a dangerous obstacle regarding his recovery. Benjamin turned his head toward Abby but didn't say a word. "Hello, Benjamin," said Abby, while she moved closer to where he was resting. "It sure is great to see you again. How are you feeling today?" asked Abby, hoping for a response of any kind. Benjamin said nothing, while he closed his eyes and turned his head away. It was obvious to Abby that Benjamin wanted nothing to do with her, but she wasn't about to leave without at least trying. She pulled up a chair and moved around to the other side of the bed. Benjamin may not have been answering her, but she knew he had to be listening. "Benjamin, I have a little something here for you," said Abby, hoping to catch Benjamin's attention. "The lady at the toy store said this was the most popular game with kids today, so I sure do hope you like it. I brought in a few other things that you may enjoy as well." Abby lifted the bag of goodies and set them at the foot of his bed. Benjamin slowly turned his head back toward Abby, opened his eyes, and smiled her way. Abby could feel the tears begin to well up in her eyes, as she thought about all the things he had been through. Although Benjamin didn't say a word, he didn't have to...his smile said it all. He was tired and afraid, but Abby knew exactly how that felt. She reached over and grabbed on to Benjamin's little hands and whispered, "It's ok, Benjamin. You're not alone. I lost my mother when I was a child just like you. There isn't a day that goes by that I don't think about her. Sweetheart, you didn't do anything wrong. I'm sure your mommy is with God right now, and He is taking good care of her. When my mother died, it took a really long time for me to understand that I will see her again someday. Once I started to realize that we would eventually be together, my sadness slowly started to go away. It didn't mean that I wasn't sad anymore. What it meant was that I knew I would see her again, and that gave me a peace that I really can't explain. One of the gifts I'm giving you today is the most important book you'll ever read. It's called a Bible, and it will help you get through the scary nights. There will be stories you read that will come to life for you...they did for me when I was little as well. At first, the Bible may not make a lot of sense to you, but don't give up. One day, the stories will seem to be written especially for you, and then you'll understand what I'm talking about here tonight. Benjamin, please let me know if you need anything at all, ok? I know what it's like to be alone and miss your mommy.

I'm here for you." And with that, Benjamin put his arms around Abby and began to sob uncontrollably. Abby leaned over and wrapped her arms around Benjamin as well... and held on just as tight as she could. Benjamin continued to squeeze her with everything he had, while Abby felt his little chest go in and out. His emotion had been building up for a very long time, and everything was now pouring out into Abby's arms. "It's ok, sweetheart. I'm here for you," said Abby, as she began to cry right along with him. Benjamin said nothing, but he didn't have to. Abby knew exactly what he was thinking...

Judge Henry Branson motioned toward the lawyers, as the final day before closing arguments was about to end. "I want to remind you, we will be moving forward with your closing arguments during tomorrow's session. I need to stress to both of you that this is my court of law; therefore, I will not permit any shenanigans. I realize the press will be asking you a lot of questions before and after the day's proceedings, but I caution you to be very careful with what you tell them. I don't want this case to be influenced by what's written in the local newspaper or what's reported on our local nightly news. This case will be decided by the facts that have been presented by the two of you. Once your closing arguments are complete, then the jury will be responsible for the final verdict. I don't want any surprises in here tomorrow, do I make myself clear?" asked Judge Branson, as he motioned toward both attorneys. "Yes, sir," responded both Abby and Mize in unison. With that, Judge Branson subsequently motioned over to the jury and asked for the foreman to come forward as well. Branson leaned over and nodded for Fletcher to move closer, stating in the process, "Mr. Fletcher, I need not tell you just how important your job is in the coming days. You're expected to keep the jury focused on the evidence and facts presented during the case. I've seen juries over the years get totally out of control, and in most cases, I put the blame solely on the shoulders of the jury foreman. My expectations of you are to lead this jury in a way that results in a decision that everyone here can be proud of, based on the evidence presented. Do you have any questions?" Fletcher nodded his head in agreement and responded, "No, sir, I don't have any questions. I'm confident we will meet your expectations." Judge Branson nodded his head in agreement and struck the gavel on the sound block in front of him declaring, "Court is now dismissed. Closing remarks will begin at 0900 tomorrow."

Chapter Nine

Closing Remarks

The doors were opened at 8:00 a.m. sharp, and the mad rush was quickly on to secure an unobstructed view of what was yet to come. The entire community had been mesmerized by the trial, as everyone involved couldn't wait to hear the closing arguments from the prosecution and the defense. There had never been a case quite like this one in the county, and the small town of Cradle Ridge would soon be feeling the impact of the outcome, whatever that may be. Abby was first to enter the courtroom, making her way over to the bench that had become her home away from home since the beginning of the trial. Looking around her, she nodded to the many familiar faces that had come to be part of the final session before the verdict was read. By the energy in the room, Abby could sense that this day was much different than the others leading up to this point. Her ability to project a confident look in the courtroom would be important; even though she knew deep down inside that a conviction would still be very difficult. This was the kind of case that could be directly impacted by the words of the two opposing lawyers, and

Abby knew it. The closing arguments would ultimately have a significant impact on the outcome, and Abby could already feel the pressure starting to mount. Abby sat down and took a deep breath. Where in the world was Mize, Abby thought, as she looked around the courtroom for her adversary? This was so like him...always trying to steal the show. Almost on queue, a buzz moved through the courtroom like a swarm of bees. Mize entered the courtroom like a heavyweight fighter, while the attendees watched on with bated breath. He played the crowd like a well-seasoned politician and methodically made his way over to the table and chair. Looking over at Abby, Mize smiled and said, "You look wonderful today, Ms. Holt. Today is going to be a terrific day for everyone involved, even you. I wish you the best." Reaching over toward Abby, Mize shook her hand, smiling the entire time. Abby extended her hand out toward Mize's crusty, old mitt and responded, "Why, thank you, Mr. Mize. I know your words are heartfelt, and I certainly do appreciate them. Good luck to you as well." Suddenly, a quiet stillness grabbed hold of the room as Judge Branson entered from just behind his desk. Everyone in the courtroom quickly rose to their feet, while Branson made it to his seat. Court was now in session...

Benjamin reached over and picked up the bag that housed the gifts from the night before. He couldn't remember the last time he had received presents of any kind, but today he would do his best to think of nothing but good thoughts. Miss Abby is a very nice woman, Benjamin thought, as he reached inside the bag once again. Out came the three super hero comic books, the baseball cards, the portable space alien video game, and the book Miss Abby had told him all about. Benjamin set all the gifts aside, except for the Bible, and he began to read the words of the book that seemed to be meant for him. At first, Benjamin wondered what Abby was talking about when she described the beauty of this book, how it would someday mean everything to him. But then…something began to change. Slowly, he turned the pages and with every word, it was as if the bitterness and sadness in his heart began to subside. Benjamin had never read anything quite like this book before, and he found himself wanting more. Miss Abby was right, he thought, as he felt a peace come over him for the first time in a very long while. Benjamin could feel something happening on the inside of his heart, and he wanted more…more of this book she called the Bible.

Abby slowly walked to the front of the courtroom and made her way to the wooden floor just in front of the jury box. Looking over at the jury, she did everything she could to put the trial's decision-makers at ease. Comfortable and surprisingly confident, Abby slowly began to present her case. The courtroom fell silent, while Abby kept her eyes focused on the faces that stared back her way. "Ladies and gentlemen of the jury, it gives me great pleasure to be with you here today. While we have spent numerous days together in this courtroom, today I am especially grateful for the opportunity to present my case to you. As all of us know, there are a number of moving parts here in this case and my opportunity to reach out and get to know each of you is limited. There have been a number of issues raised by both myself and Mr. Mize, but the most important takeaway for all of us is the impact this accident had on a little boy. Think about how your life would have been different than it is today if you grew up without parents. When Benjamin's mother was tragically killed by Edward Conners's negligence, Benjamin Sanders became an orphan…pure and simple. This little boy's life will never be the same because the love of his life, the only person who mattered to him, was taken away from him just when he needed her the most. Since the accident, Benjamin has gone into a shell. He is housed up in a facility that is nothing more than a halfway house for orphans, while he waits for a designated foster home to be identified. The state has decided to keep him in this protective custody, hoping that he will somehow snap out of his current frame of mind and move on with his life. Are you kidding me! We're talking about a seven-year-old little boy…who is now all alone. Let's think back on the night in question, when Mr. Conners slammed his car into Olivia Sanders. She was parked on the side of the road, and that is when Mr. Conners lost control of his vehicle and took her out. Little Benjamin miraculously made it through the accident, but his mother was tragically killed and here we are trying to pick up the pieces. Regardless of what you decide, ladies and gentlemen of the jury, we will all leave the courtroom after this trial. All of us will depart to the safety of our own homes, and we will quickly move on with our lives. Benjamin, on the other hand, will not have this luxury. He has no idea who his family will be, and where he will live. This is what I want all of you to focus on...the face of a little boy who may never have joy in his heart again. I can only hope and pray that the message you send through your verdict of guilty will be heard throughout this country. The courage you show as members of this jury will be a strong one for all to emulate...that we simply cannot allow for this kind of ignorance to continue. I ask that you bring back a verdict of guilty. Maybe, just maybe, it will keep this from ever happening again. Thank you." Abby turned and made her way back to her chair. Oh, how she wanted to look over toward Mize, but she knew it was more important for her to capture the support of the courtroom's attendees instead. She knew it was dangerous for her to only play the emotional card, but deep down inside, Abby knew this was about all she had. The evidence against Conners was shaky at best, and she knew there was a strong probability that Mize would quickly rip apart her strategy. The courtroom fell silent, as all eyes were now focused on the man who was about to take center stage. Mize reached for his glasses, slid them on to the bridge of his nose, and looked directly into the eyes of the jury. Mize was ready to deliver his message, but was the courtroom prepared for what was about to come their way?

Mize began to move toward the jury box, and it was obvious to everyone seated in the courtroom that he was indeed an expert on the power of persuasion. Without ever saying a word, Mize immediately demanded respect from all parties involved, as he moved closer to the front of the room. His ability to connect with his audience was a cut above all others in his field, and he began to position himself for the spotlight he desired. Mize could feel the eyes of the jury staring his way, which only made him stronger. He took a deep breath and began to shake his head, as he captivated the recipients of his upcoming message. Mize's lesson was about to begin. "Ladies and gentlemen of this illustrious jury. I am Warren Mize. . . the most celebrated and experienced attorney in this area. I represent the defendant, Mr. Edward Conners, here today. While I've been a part of nearly every major case here in beautiful Epoch County, I honestly don't believe I've ever been part of a case quite like this one. This is my first opportunity to match wits with Ms. Holt over here, and I do admit that I've been very impressed with her courtroom savvy. In fact, I hate to say it, but there's a part of me that's really missing old Ben Joulson right about now." Laughter broke out in the courtroom, as Mize continued with his rambling monologue. Abby turned around and watched the courtroom audience chuckle at Joulson's expense. What in the world was Mize up to, Abby thought, as she tried to assess the emotional temperature of the courtroom that surrounded her. "When I first agreed to take on this case, I had no idea who in the world Edward Conners was," continued Mize, as he pointed over to where his client was seated. "We initially sat down and discussed the details surrounding the events of the night in question, and he made it very clear to me that he did nothing wrong. I told Mr. Conners that I never take on a case if there is any possibility that I will compromise my integrity in searching for the truth. The fact of the matter is that my client was telling me the truth beginning on day one. He did nothing wrong. Think about the frame of mind any of us would have been in had we been the ones who just lost a close friend like Edward Conners did. We would have been doing a whole lot more than speeding on the night in question, I can tell you that much!" And with that, Mize stepped back and caught his breath, as if something had just slipped out of his mouth without prior approval. "I mean," Mize continued, "there's not a one of us here in this court-room that wouldn't have been shook up as well." Edward leaned forward in his seat and reached for his glass of water, trying to maintain the composure that was quickly deserting him. What in the world did Mize just say, Edward thought, as he replayed the words in his head once again. Abby looked over at the jury and could only hope that Mize's last line didn't go unnoticed. Mize quickly moved on to a new train of thought, but there was no doubt in anyone's mind that he was quickly losing control of the courtroom he had owned just a few moments before. "Ladies and gentlemen of the jury, I ask that each of you search from within when you finalize your decision regarding this trial. It will be extremely important for you to work as a team so that justice can be served. I thank you for your service, and I'm confident you will send a message to this courtroom that when you took an oath to serve Epoch County and this wonderful country of ours, you took your job very seriously. Thank you." Mize turned his back on the jury and made his way to his seat. Without lifting his eyes either toward the jury or in the direction of his client,

Mize simply stared forward and waited for Judge Branson's final instructions.

The courtroom fell silent, while Branson made a motion for the jury to stand. "Ladies and gentlemen of the jury, you have a tremendous responsibility when you leave this courtroom today. It will be very important for you to stay sequestered in your room while you are here on these premises and not have any discussion with anyone other than your peers on the jury. When you leave this courtroom, it will also be equally important to refrain from having any discussion with anyone outside this court of law about the case including anything that happens during the deliberation process. You will put this entire case at risk if you do not follow these strict guidelines, and I will not tolerate this at any juncture during this decision-making process. If any of you breach this contract of secrecy, I promise you that you'll have to answer to me. Do I make myself clear?" "Yes, sir," mouthed the jury, while they nodded their heads in agreement. "Good," responded Branson. "Please, follow Mr. Winters over here through the door, and he will take you to your conference room. Hopefully, the accommodations will suit you just fine. Thanks in advance for all you are doing. I'm sure you will make the right decision. Court is now adjourned."

Edward leaned over and whispered into Mize's ear, "As soon as we get outside, I want to speak with you. You and I have some talkin' to do." Mize smiled back at Edward and responded, "Sounds like a plan, Edward. Don't look so worried. You look like you just saw a ghost or something.

Everything's going to be just fine." Abby looked on from a distance and could see obvious dissention taking over the camp of her greatest adversary. In a matter of minutes, she could almost feel the momentum of the case swing from Mize over to her side. Abby's intuitiveness kicked in, while she replayed the events since the day's opening bell. For whatever reason, it was as if Mize had fumbled the ball at the one-yard line after leading for the entire game. Abby watched the jurors leave their box and couldn't help but wonder what would happen behind closed doors. She also knew there would be dozens of reporters waiting for her outside the doors of the courtroom, hoping to get a glimpse of the key players from the morning session. Abby pushed her way through the crowd and on into the hallway that led away from the courtroom. As she opened the door, the first of many microphones waited for her arrival. "Ms. Holt, Charlotte Seavers from WJES station here in Cradle Ridge. How do you think the jury will assess the closing arguments delivered by you and Mr. Mize? From the initial feedback that has already made its way to us, it sounds like you more than held your own with the brash attorney. How do you think you did?" Abby stopped and looked into the camera, knowing that her response would more than likely be on the late news that evening. "I do believe we have a very knowledgeable group of jurors here representing Epoch County, and I'm confident they will make the right decision when all is said and done. Let's just say that I'm very happy with the way the session ended today. There was no doubt

in anyone's mind that the momentum in this case came over
to our side toward the latter stages of the trial. I'm confident
this will be verified when the final verdict is read. I feel very
good about our chances." Two steps later and another surge
of reporters practically pushed her up against the building.
"Chance Detrick, WTZA station from just across the river in
Meadow Gulch," said the voice attached to the microphone
that pressed up against her left cheek. "Do you realize that
it's been almost four years since Warren Mize has lost a case
here in Epoch County? Do you honestly think you beat him,
Ms. Holt, considering the fact that a number of other attorneys with a whole lot more experience than you have under
your belt, have been slaughtered by this guy? What makes
you think you're better than them?" Abby took a few more
steps and then realized it would be a whole lot better for
her to make one general statement, rather than continue to
answer all these questions separately. Only two steps out of
the courtroom and she was already worn out. Abby stopped
and looked into the cameras once again, making it clear to all
that this would be her final statement of the day. Otherwise,
she may never get home. "Folks, first of all, I appreciate all
of your support over the past couple of months. You've been
respectful to both myself and my client, and for that, I am
grateful. I honestly don't feel like I'm better than anybody.
Mr. Mize is an excellent attorney...truly one of the finest
in the entire country. But this case is not about the lawyers,
including Mize or myself. I honestly don't believe that I did
anything special; the facts of the case did all the necessary

talking during the trial. Tonight, I'm going to go home and try to get some rest. This has been a very exhausting trial for all of us because it's a case that has captured the attention of everyone here in this county. It shows all of us that our lives can be altered in a matter of seconds. When this change is brought on because of one's negligence and others are hurt in the process, then someone has to suffer the consequences. This case truly exemplifies the fragility of life, something that none of us can ever take for granted. I'm confident the upcoming verdict will impact all of us one way or the other. As I said before, I feel very good about our chances, but not because of what I did. As the days went on, the facts of this case surfaced, which is something you hope for at any trial. Thanks again for being so supportive. I really do appreciate it." With that, Abby made her way for the door and quickly ran down the steps of the courthouse. Within seconds, she was across the street and into the city park. There would be no ride waiting for Abby, but that was just fine. The walk felt good, as the brisk air against her face brought a sense of peace that she hadn't felt in a very long time. Closing her eyes, she could still see Benjamin's smile when he opened the packages she had brought to his room. Their connection was real, and she couldn't wait to see him again.

Mize and Edward ran toward the limousine in the front of the courthouse, brushing off the droves of reporters who followed close behind. Screams from the local television personalities were directed their way, while they reached for the unlocked door of the ride that awaited their arrival. The reporters smelled blood and circled the two of them like a pack of hungry wolves, but they moved quickly and were just out of their reach. They jumped into the limo and slammed the door, as the reporters were less than five feet behind them. Tapping Thomas on the right shoulder, Mize said, "Let's get out of here, Thomas. I've seen enough of these pathetic parasites today. I need to get home and have a glass of wine." Edward interrupted Mize before he could utter another word, "What in the world were you doing in there today, Mize? You completely screwed up this case and everything we had done up to the closing remarks. You bumbled and stumbled your way through some meaningless, pompous gibberish that accomplished nothing other than to make Ms. Holt look like the attorney of the year. What in the world were you thinking, Mize? The only thing that anyone is going to remember from your closing remarks is that I was supposedly speeding when I hit her car. You know that's not true and it's never been communicated at the trial, up until today. You screwed up big time, Mize. All we can hope for now is that the jury wasn't paying attention to your mistake because if they were, our case is in big trouble." Mize listened but didn't say a word. Finally, he tapped Thomas on the shoulder again and responded, "Thomas, could you please drop Mr. Conners off up here at the corner, so he can get a cab? I think that would be the best thing for both of us right now." "Sure thing, boss," replied Thomas. "Not a problem." Thomas veered into the right lane and made his way to the corner. Edward looked over at Mize and said, "That's it, Mize. You're going to drop me off here. After all we've been through, this is the way you treat me?" Mize took out his wallet and reached for a twenty dollar bill. Throwing it toward Edward, Mize said, "This should cover your cab ride home, Conners. Now, get out of here." Edward slowly made his way out of the car, while Thomas quickly sped off and left him standing on the corner alone. Thomas glanced up at the mirror and caught a glimpse of Mize's face. Their eyes met, and both men couldn't help but smile at the events of the day. Everything was falling into place very nicely...

Chapter Ten

The Decision

T he jury made their way into the large boardroom and knew this would be their new home until a final verdict was reached. Even though the accommodations were more than adequate and the refreshments were plentiful, all members of the jury knew the responsibility they had was enormous. Their personal identity was known to nearly every inhabitant of Epoch County, and the verdict they ultimately reached would undoubtedly be debated for years. The impact had taken a toll on every member of the jury and all were eager to get started, none more anxious than the jury foreman, Richard Fletcher. Fletcher quickly made his way to the head of the table, while the rest of the jury picked an open seat. "First of all, I want to thank all of you in advance for your commendable teamwork," said Fletcher, as he looked out at the other 11 members of the jury. "This trial has had a huge impact on each and every one of us, so I think it's safe to say that we all want to come to a decision regarding this case as quickly as possible. Having said that, we also want to make sure we ultimately make the right decision. This is the most important thing of all. We need to do what's right. There are a couple of things we need to focus on very closely. The charge that has been brought up against Edward Conners is vehicular manslaughter, which can reflect factors like drunk and reckless driving, excessive speeding, gross negligence, etc. To me, this case is pretty cut and dry. Do we believe Edward Conners was negligent and, as a result, caused the death of Olivia Sanders? If we do, then he's guilty. If we don't believe he was negligent, then he walks free. I don't know how we could ever think he wasn't negligent, but I'm certainly open for discussion regarding the charges. His odd behavior after the death of his friend, coupled with the fact that he was going way too fast when he hit Olivia Sanders's parked car, makes this a pretty easy case to decide. The only thing we really need to take a look at is whether this is a felony or a misdemeanor. If we want Mr. Conners to get off with a year or less, then his act of negligence was merely a misdemeanor. If not, it was a felony. All 12 of us need to agree on the verdict or Conners could receive an acquittal, which means he walks scot-free. Obviously, we don't want this to happen." Fletcher looked around the table, almost daring anyone on the jury to challenge him. "Mr. Fletcher, I don't think we want to rush to any decision," replied Tobias Wells, known to the group as juror number four. "We should talk about every single issue and then decide the fate of Mr. Conners. We must not rush to judgment, one way or the other." Fletcher felt his face begin to turn flush, while he did all he could to politely acknowledge the peanut gallery to his right. "You're absolutely right, Mr. Wells," responded Fletcher. "We need to make sure we don't miss anything." With that, Fletcher sat back in his seat. He had a feeling this was going to be a very long night...

Benjamin's entire schedule started to revolve around the book that was slowly working on his heart. Since his mother's passing, Benjamin's life had been completely turned upside down. The only thing that seemed to help him with the pain he was going through was the Bible given to him from Abby. He found himself thinking about the one person who was doing everything she could to help him since the accident. When would Miss Abby be coming back to see me, Benjamin thought, as he continued to read the stories that were suddenly coming to life. He couldn't wait to sit down and show her just how much he had read since she dropped off his present. He continued to read and turn the pages at record pace, while he thought about how some of the stories in the book mimicked his life. Miss Abby really did seem to care about how Benjamin was doing, and this was something that was very new to him. Everyone else was only concerned with getting him placed with another family, and this made him sad and afraid. When he did read the Bible, he temporarily forgot about his painful past and began to focus his mind on the future. For whatever reason, this is what the Bible did for him. It made him realize that he was loved, which was something he had given up on when his mother died. The feeling of peace in his heart was coming back once again, and Benjamin had no doubt in his mind that it was because of the Bible he had been given. Of all the gifts that he had received, this was his favorite present of all.

"Come on folks, we're into this discussion five hours now, and we're not making any progress," said Fletcher, as he looked out at the 11 sets of tired eyes around the table. "Is there anyone here who doesn't think Edward Conners is responsible for the death of Olivia Sanders? We need to see your hand if you think he had nothing at all to do with her death." Everyone looked around the room to see if anyone was willing to stand up to Fletcher, but nobody raised their hand. Just as Fletcher was about to move on and finalize the jury's decision, Tobias Wells raised his hand. He wasn't about to go down that easily. Fletcher could feel the hairs on the back of his neck stand up, as he motioned for Wells to speak up. "Mr. Fletcher, I appreciate the fact that you want us to come to a quick decision, but I'm just not sure it's as easy as you say. We really don't know if Edward Conners did anything wrong on the night in question. All we know is that he was there and…" Fletcher had heard enough and could sense that Wells was beginning to have an impact on the rest of the jury. He needed to stop this before it took hold. "Mr. Wells, I think we've had a very long day today," interrupted Fletcher. "I think we should call it a day and pick this discussion up in the morning. I'm sure everyone here wants to hear your opinion but it's really getting late. Let's all go home tonight and get some rest. I'm sure tomorrow is going to be a very long day." The jurors nodded their heads in agreement, as they watched Fletcher reach for his briefcase. Tobias was stopped in the middle of his sentence and could sense that his pushback was not well-received by Fletcher. Maybe Fletcher was right, Tobias thought, as he mentally assessed the events of the day. It may make sense to tackle these issues first thing in the morning after a good night's rest...

Edward slammed the door behind him, as he made his way into his front room. Three beers and a shot of bourbon after his day in the courtroom only contributed to the foul mood he was in after Mize's closing arguments. Edward's stomach was in knots, while he thought about the bizarre change of events toward the end of the trial. Mize's transformation from one of the best attorneys Edward had ever seen into a bumbling fool was almost hard to believe. As good as he was throughout the entire trial, he was equally as bad during the closing session. What on earth happened to Mize, Edward thought, as he began to shake at the thought of what was yet to come. Edward reached over and grabbed his cell phone from the table. Mize's name was seven clicks down on his speed dial, and Edward hit the number from memory. Oh, how he desperately needed to speak with Mize to find out what to do next. This sitting around and wondering what his future would hold was more than he could handle, and Edward waited for Mize's voice to come to the line. His confidence was shattered after the day's events, as Edward could feel the life he so dearly coveted begin to vanish before his eyes. Mize's phone called out his name, but on this particular night, there was no reason for him to answer. "Warren, are you going to get the phone?" the woman asked. Looking down at his cell phone, Mize saw Edward's name blinking his way. Mize had no time for him tonight because he had better things to do with his time than subject himself to Edward's incessant whimpering. "Honey, it's only Conners. Nothing important, I'm sure," said Mize, while he looked over at the woman who had quickly become a major part of his life. "There's really not much I can say to him right now except that his life is in for a big change...a change he's not going to like one bit!" And with that, the woman set her drink down and started to laugh. She'd been dreaming about this night for a very long time, and soon it would finally be here. In her own little world of paybacks, justice was about to be served.

Tobias made his way into the conference room, as he and the rest of the jurors got settled in for another long day. Reaching for his briefcase, he thought about where their discussion had ended the night before, and where he was when Fletcher rudely cut him off. As Tobias opened his briefcase, he could feel his stomach immediately flip upside down, while he stared at the picture that was resting on his notes. There they were...his wife and two beautiful girls, with a red "X" marked through their faces. Tobias turned the picture over and read the note meant for him..."Nice family Wells. Change your position today and they won't get hurt. This is not a joke. Don't test me". Tobias felt a ball of sweat immediately form on his forehead, and he quickly shut his briefcase. Looking up from the picture that had just sent chills down the back of his neck, his eyes were met by those of

Fletcher. It was obvious by the look staring back his way that Fletcher was the author of the message left behind. Tobias felt a lump in his throat start to form, and he tried desperately to swallow. He started to choke and grabbed for the glass of water in front of him. "Are you going to be okay, Mr. Wells?" asked Fletcher, as he lifted the pitcher to refresh his empty glass. "Yes, I'll be fine," answered Tobias. "Good, then let's get started," replied Fletcher, while he quickly moved into the morning session. "Now, where were we last night when our meeting ended? Mr. Wells, I believe you were starting to talk about Mr. Conners and the night in question. What was it that you wanted to say?" Tobias looked over at Fletcher, knowing full well what his expectations were. No matter how hard he tried, he just couldn't get the picture of his family out of his mind. It was obvious to him that lives were at risk depending on the answer he was about to give. Nothing was more important to Tobias than his family...his feedback to Fletcher and the group would need to be succinct and direct.

"Mr. Fletcher, I've been thinking about this case all night long," stated Tobias. "In fact, I don't think I slept a wink from the time I went to bed until the time I got up just a few hours ago. Without any doubt in my mind, I do believe Olivia Sanders is dead because Edward Conners was irresponsible in his actions. The fact of the matter is that his speeding and negligence had a direct impact on her death. We need to send a strong message to everyone in Epoch County that this kind of behavior cannot be tolerated, no matter what your financial status is. His actions, in my humble opinion, warrant a felony conviction." Fletcher could almost feel a smile begin to form on his seasoned face, but he held back...at least for now. Turning to the rest of the jury, Fletcher jumped at the opportunity to close the deal. "Is there anyone here who disagrees with Mr. Wells? I think he makes some very good points," stated Fletcher. Fletcher waited to see if anyone objected and then moved quickly for resolution. "It looks like we have all come to a decision. On our behalf, I will let the court know that we're ready to communicate our verdict to all parties involved." Fletcher sat down and looked over at Tobias. Neither of them said anything...they didn't have to. Both of them knew exactly what the other one was thinking.

Word spread quickly to both legal teams that a decision had been made, and all respective individuals were notified to get to the courthouse for the rendering of the decision. Abby could feel her heart begin to race, as she began to think about all the possible scenarios that were in front of her. After getting the word, Mize dialed Edward's number to let him know it was time. Edward's life was about to change...one way or the other. "Conners, this is Mize. I just got the call indicating that the jury has finalized their decision, which means we need to be at the courthouse at 4:00 p.m. this afternoon. I'll be getting there just before the announcement because I have other meetings that will be running right up until that time. Why don't we just meet there at about 3:45 p.m. and we'll go in together?" "Wait just a minute, Mize," replied Edward. "Don't hang up. This is a quick verdict. What do you think it means?" Conners waited for an answer, while

Mize purposely allowed the silence to play tricks with his client's head. Mize thought about hanging up but couldn't miss out on an opportunity like this. "Conners, I don't think it means anything, good or bad," answered Mize, in a non-chalant way. "I have had verdicts go one way or the other. I guess we'll just have to wait and see." Edward could feel his blood begin to boil, while he played back the words of his illustrious lawyer. Mize had a feeling his feedback would have this kind of effect on Edward, and he certainly wasn't disappointed. "What do you mean, we'll just have to wait and see!" screamed Edward. "What happened to the cocky lawyer who took on my case? You sound like you've con-ceited the decision and you're expecting defeat. I sure hope you're a better business partner than you are a lawyer!" And with that, Mize could hold back no more. Laughter soon muffled the words of Edward, as Mize found himself speech-less due to the temporary hysteria that replaced his response. "Oh, Edward," replied Mize. "You're even more gullible than I originally thought. See you in the courtroom at 4:00 today." Edward dropped the phone in disbelief and fell to the floor. How in the world did he ever let this happen...

"All rise, the court is now in session," said the bailiff, as the courthouse fell silent in anticipation of the decision that was about to come their way. "The honorable Judge Branson now presiding." "Ladies and gentlemen, we gather here today to hear the jury's decision regarding the case of Epoch County versus Edward Conners," announced Judge Branson, as he set the stage for the verdict that would soon send shock waves throughout the county. "Realizing that this case has garnered as much local and national attention as any case we've ever seen in this county, I want to preface the upcoming decision by stating that I will not tolerate any unruly behavior after the verdict is announced. If any of you don't believe me, just try me. I will hold you in contempt of this court, and you will be the next one on trial here in my courtroom. I hope I make myself clear. This goes for everyone in this room today, including the press. Now, Mr. Fletcher, are you ready to share your decision with this courtroom today?" "I am, your honor," replied Fletcher, as he began to approach the bench. Fletcher handed the verdict to Branson, and without any reaction whatsoever, he read the decision to himself. Handing it back to Fletcher, Judge Branson stated, "You may now communicate this decision to the court." Fletcher turned and faced the rows of people in front of him. "Ladies and gentlemen of this courtroom, we the jury, find Edward Conners guilty of involuntary manslaughter; his negligence directly resulting in the death of Olivia Sanders," announced Fletcher, while the courtroom immediately erupted in disarray and atypical frenzy. With no regard for what Judge Branson had just said, cameras and bodies quickly made their way to where Conners was standing. Mize grabbed his briefcase and coat and quickly bolted for the door. Before Edward knew it, he was all alone with an abundance of microphones jammed in his face. "Mr. Conners, Mr. Conners," screamed the throngs of reporters who immediately moved in for the kill. "Do you think justice has been served here today? What kind of sentence do you think you'll receive when the terms are announced? How does it feel to be on the receiving end of a guilty verdict?"

Edward began to push his way through the crowd and searched frantically for Mize, who was already out the side door. Waiting for Mize in the parking lot, adjacent to the courthouse, was a gathering of reporters. Recognizing a number of them from past interaction over the years, Mize made his way down to where they were waiting. The setting was perfect for him, as he was now in a position to make a statement that would be captured by all. No longer was he in a reactive fishbowl inside the courtroom...he had much more control over the content of his statement, which was exactly what he wanted. "On behalf of my client, Edward Conners, I want everyone to know that we are gravely disappointed with the court's decision today," stated Mize, as he looked directly into the swarms of cameras pointed his way. "This decision was based on emotion, not on fact, and we will be more than likely appealing this decision in the coming months. My client, Edward Conners, is a good man and what happened to him today is a travesty. I have no further comment...not right now." Mize plowed through the reporters and made his way over to where Thomas had parked their limousine. Jumping in, he slammed the door behind him and motioned for Thomas to drive off. Within minutes, they had made their way to the main thoroughfare. Mize reached for the phone and dialed the number from memory. "How did it go?" asked the voice on the other end of the line. "Perfect," answered Mize, as he poured himself a glass of wine in the back of the car. "Everything we've discussed is in place." And with that, Mize closed his eyes and took a sip of his wine. Never in his life had it ever tasted so good...

Chapter Eleven

The Final Wish

"Mize, this Edward. You've been avoiding me since the verdict was read last week. I want you to know that I've posted bail, and I'm now a free man, at least for the time being…no thanks to you. This means that you and I need to talk about our little agreement," said Edward, as he continued to talk into the recorder that seemed to be mocking his every word. "I need you to call me back as soon as possible so we can finalize a plan regarding our new company. We both know that my investment of $10M is now in your hands, so I expect full cooperation on your part. If you don't agree to see me in the next few days, then I will go straight to the press. I will expose everything, and we will both go down. I have nothing to lose right now, but you do. Click." Mize sat and listened to Edward's voice over his recorder and contemplated his next move. Final sentencing for Edward would be in less than a month, which meant that Mize would have to keep Edward at bay for at least that time. Somehow, he had to tap into the desperation that was evident in Edward's voice and use it to his advantage. Mize thought through the sequence of events one more time, and then it came to him. He reached down and grabbed his cell phone. It was time to accelerate the final phase of his plan, as Mize could sense that everything accomplished up to this point was now at risk. "We need to meet tonight," said Mize, as he spoke softly into the phone. "I need you to expedite the final wish for Conners or everything could be exposed. We can't be seen by anyone so let's meet at the shed, behind mile marker 113. You better make sure you're not followed by anyone. 9:00 o'clock tonight...be there." Mize closed his cell phone and thought about what needed to be done in order to walk away with everything. He could almost taste the $10M, but he also knew the volatility of the situation he was in. He was either going to walk away with all the marbles...or nothing. Everything done up to this point had worked perfectly because he was able to tap into Edward's greatest downfall, which was greed. He could only hope that this mindset would not change, as the final chapter in his plan was ready to begin.

Abby tossed and turned in her bed, while she continued to think back on the events of the trial. Although she was grateful for the final verdict, something just didn't feel right about how everything had played out. Something was missing, and this was the issue that continued to wreak havoc with her mind. Abby had beaten Mize at his own game, humiliated him in front of his hometown peers, yet he seemed to be taking the loss in stride. He had entered the courtroom on day one with an intensity that was unlike anything she'd ever seen before, but that look was nowhere to be found on the day of the closing arguments. Mize's undisputed reputation was to win at all costs; however, this certainly didn't seem to be the case at all regarding the Edward Conners trial. No matter how hard Abby tried to focus on the final outcome and the events leading up to this point, she continually found herself coming back to Benjamin. There was something about this little boy, something that captured Abby's attention ever since the first day she met him. Although Benjamin had never spoken a word to anyone since he lost his mother, Abby's prayer every night was that she would somehow find a way to reach him. Every time she looked into his blue eyes, she thought about her own father and what he meant to her...how he had helped ease the horrific pain she was going through when she lost her mother and sister. Abby could sense a much different Benjamin the last time she visited him, as a peace had moved into his heart despite all he pain he had suffered. While Abby had done all she could to avoid the night that turned his world upside down, she knew it would be important for him to revisit that night one more time. She felt a strong sense of urgency to get to Benjamin now that the trial had ended because she knew he would be leaving soon. His move into a foster home would be accelerated, and Abby had no doubt in her mind that she was dealing with borrowed time. It was time for her to see him again...before it was too late.

Mize parked his car and ran down to the end of the street, disappearing into the darkness just behind mile marker 113.

Off in the distance, he could see the shed that awaited his arrival. Although he did all he could to avoid this place, this meeting was unavoidable and Mize knew it. If Conners went to the press now, it would jeopardize everything that had been done up to this point, and Mize's plan would fall apart at the seams. He made his way down the path and could see the light waiting for him in the back of the shed. Mize opened the door and proceeded to move his way toward the dark, musty room where the light originated. Celeste was sitting in her chair, waiting for Mize's arrival. "Celeste, we need to implement a slight modification to our plan. I received a call from Conners, and he is starting to panic. This is understandable, in light of the current circumstances. I need you to get in contact with Conners right away and agree to meet with him. You tell him that his third wish will be granted by you a bit earlier than anticipated, due to a change in your schedule. I really don't care what you tell him, but you need to find a way to meet him for that final wish. The key to making this work, Celeste, is your ability to once again tap into the greed factor that has been his primary focus for a long time now. His first two wishes were focused on his own personal gain, and that played right into our hands. His third wish needs to have the same impact. The guy will be going to prison soon, and once that happens, his word will mean nothing. He will be viewed as some babbling lunatic when he tries to explain how he lost the $10M handed over to him from Ridgeley. What you need to do is get him to focus on a third wish that buys us some time. You've done a good job of getting him this far, but everything moving forward depends on the timing of the third wish. He has way too much riding on this final stage, so now it's just a matter of implementing this last step of our plan. Don't mess up, Celeste, or you will not live to see another day. That...I promise you. As soon as you finish with him, you get yourself over to the cottage. The entire committee will be waiting for you when you arrive. We need to know exactly what transpires with Conners during your visit." Celeste looked up at Mize's imposing figure and could see the veins on his forehead protrude with his every breath. She had heard stories about Mize over the years when things didn't go his way, and she knew by the look in his eyes that his threats were real. "I will make sure it happens," answered Celeste. "I understand what's expected, and I will make sure his final wish fits into our plan." Mize nodded his head in agreement and leaned down with one more message for Celeste, "You let me know as soon as you're finished. I want to be ready for Conners in case he decides to do something stupid."

Abby made her way to the 4th Floor and was soon inside Benjamin's room. Her visit was unannounced, and Benjamin's face lit up the minute she entered his quarters. His Bible rested next to him, and Abby could tell immediately by his reaction that he had been moved by the book that was changing his life right in front of her eyes. Abby made her way over to Benjamin's bed and sat down next to him. His little hands reached out for Abby and quickly held on with all he had. Abby could feel his love pour out on her, while she continued to hold on to him as well. Never before had she ever felt anything quite like this, as the little boy's heart had literally opened up and let her in. "Benjamin, I'm so happy to see you today. I've been thinking about you a lot lately, and I just want you to know that I'm here for you. The staff told me that you're going to be leaving soon. It sounds like there are some very nice places you may be going to, and I just wanted to make sure I saw you before you left." Benjamin's smile immediately left his face, as Abby's words had brought the reality of his situation to the forefront once again. How could I be so stupid, Abby thought, as she found herself scrambling to somehow find the joy that had disappeared right in front of her eyes. Benjamin reached over and grabbed his Bible and held it to his chest, as tears began to flow down his little, red cheeks. Abby gently put her hands up to Benjamin's face and began to wipe his tears away. "Benjamin, it's going to be ok. You can talk to me. I'm here to listen and help make the pain go away. Tell me what happened with your mother. I want to help you."

The door bell rang and Edward slowly made his way to the front door. He may have been out on bail, but Edward Conners had become a prisoner in his own house. No matter where he went, he could feel the eyes of the community watch his every move. He needed to get to Mize before it was too late. He opened the door and immediately became fixated on the handwritten note attached to his screen door. Edward looked up and down the street, but whoever left the note was already gone. The letters on the note looked familiar, and within a few seconds, it was obvious to Edward that he had seen them before. Edward shut the door behind him and sat down to read the message solely intended for him…

Dear Mr. Conners:

I've been called out of the country on assignment and will be unable to fulfill your third and final wish in the time frame we initially agreed to. However, I will be available to implement this final stage of our agreement tomorrow evening at 9:00 p.m. if you're interested. I realize this is short notice, but I have no other choice. I will be at the shed waiting for you when you arrive, should you decide to move forward. If you're not there, I will understand.

Bye for now…
Celeste

Edward's mind began to race, as he quickly gathered his thoughts. His life had been totally flipped upside down since the last time he met with Celeste, and he was quickly running out of options. The timing of Celeste's note brought even more uncertainty to Edward, and he could sense that there was a lot more to it than she was leading on to. Why in the world would she show up now with this "all or nothing proposal" regarding their final visit? Edward felt his pulse begin to race, while he thought back through the sequence of events that led up to the guilty verdict that came his way. He needed to think through the meeting that was about to take place because he had a feeling that this could be the last time he saw Celeste. Somehow, he had to uncover the answers he so desperately needed, and Celeste was the key. Edward went into his study and began to write down everything that had happened since the night of the accident. He had to find a way to get his arms around the upcoming meeting with Celeste. This woman had surfaced out of nowhere and taken hold of his life, and now he needed to find out why. He had to get to the bottom of this before it was too late. One thing was for certain…he was running out of time.

Benjamin looked up at Abby and nodded his head in agreement. She could see in his eyes that he trusted her, and she waited for his words to flow. She waited, and then out came the soft voice that immediately captivated her heart. "Miss Abby, thanks for being my friend," said Benjamin, as his mind began to take him back to the night that changed everything. Abby moved closer to Benjamin and took a deep breath, while she mentally prepared herself for the words that were about to come her way. "I remember the night with my mommy real well. She had picked me up that day at my school, and we went out for some ice cream. She and I both liked chocolate the best because it made us feel like we were eating candy. We sat in our favorite spot on the patio and just talked about fun things. Miss Abby, it was my best day ever. My mommy was my best friend, and she always made me feel loved. We left the ice cream store just before dark because we had a pretty long ride home. I remember falling asleep in the car, just like I usually did. The next thing I knew, we were stopped on the side of the road. I remember waking up and my mommy was holding her chest because she was having a hard time breathing. I didn't know what to do, and I was afraid. She fell asleep in my arms and didn't wake up. The last thing she did was hand me her necklace with the locket, and then she was gone. This was my most special gift from her, Miss Abby. I should have done something for her when she was trying to catch her breath, but I just didn't know what to do, Miss Abby. I didn't know what to do."

Benjamin buried his head into Abby's shoulder and began to sob. Abby wiped away his tears and did all she could to console him. "Benjamin, it's ok. You didn't do anything wrong, honey. There was nothing you could have done. After your mommy fell asleep, then what did you do next?" Benjamin gathered his thoughts and regained his composure, while he painfully took himself back to the memory of his mother lying on the seat of the car. "Miss Abby, I reached over and touched my mommy's face, but it didn't move. I asked her to wake up, but she didn't hear me. I was real scared and got out of the car and started to walk away, but I didn't know where to go. Before I knew it, there was a car heading right at me, and all I remember was a big crash. The car stopped on the road and out walked a man toward me. I kind of remember him asking me some questions, but all I could think about was my mommy's face back in the car. I don't remember much after that except driving away with a bunch of strangers. Lights were everywhere, and my mommy was gone. That's all I remember. After that, everything was just a blur and then everyone was asking me all sorts of questions. My best friend in the whole wide world was gone. Up until you gave me that Bible, nothing really seemed to matter to me anymore, and I wanted to die so I could be with her again. You're really the only friend I have, Miss Abby. Now, I have all these people coming into my room telling me they're going to send me to a real nice place with lots of kids. I don't want to go, Miss Abby. I just want to be with my mommy. That's all I really want." Abby did all she could to stay strong, but Benjamin's story hit her right between the eyes. As she listened to his little voice, she remembered the loss of her sister and mother and knew exactly what he was talking about. Through a series of personal tragedies, God had brought the two of them together. It was clear to her that Benjamin's journey had taken him directly into Abby's path, and she was grateful for her newfound, little friend. Suddenly, she thought about what Benjamin had just told her…and her heart fell straight to the floor! Her mind began to race, as she replayed Benjamin's soft, little words. She put her hands to her face and gasped for air…

Edward took a deep breath and looked out into the darkness that awaited him. Deep down inside, he knew his meeting with Celeste could potentially lead him to the answers he so desperately needed right now. He made his way past mile marker 113 and quickly disappeared into the darkness. He entered through the open door, gathered his bearings, and found Celeste waiting for him in the corner of the back room once again. There was a chair sitting next to the left side of the table, and he sat down and waited for her to make the first move. "Mr. Conners, by now you know the drill. You have one more wish, assuming you decide to exercise it. I'll be leaving the country so you need to make your decision tonight. I must caution you that your third wish will go into effect when you wake up in the morning." Edward thought about how he wanted to respond. He needed to test Celeste to see if she was legitimate or not…so he quickly jumped on her offer for his third and final wish. "I've been thinking about my third wish, and I've decided not to move forward on it. There's really nothing left for me to wish for, so I think I'm going to pass. When I drove down here tonight, I had something in mind but that has changed. I'm going to leave now."

Edward began to get out of his chair; however, his departure was quickly interrupted by Celeste's voice from the corner of the room. This was the sign he was waiting for because it told him what he needed to know. Now, Edward would play along with the game, hoping it would lead him to the source behind his rapid spiral downward. "Mr. Conners, wait right there before you go any further," responded Celeste, as she leaned out from behind the darkness. "Are you sure you don't want that third wish? I mean, there has to be something you want, isn't there?" Edward turned and made his way back to the chair. "You're right, Celeste. There is something I would like to see happen. My sentencing is coming up next month, and I'd like to get off on a misdemeanor charge with minimal probation as my penalty. This will allow me to move forward with my life and secure the plan that was put into place quite some time ago." Celeste nodded her head and responded, "Your wish will go into effect tomorrow, and everything will be put in place for minimal sentencing. However, it will be very important for you stay low and not have contact with anyone until this is communicated. That way, you'll be assured of catching everyone off guard with the announcement. You should not say anything to anyone about this before the sentencing is read. You may go now."

Edward got up and made his way out the front door and walked swiftly over to his car. He drove away and quickly veered off the side of the road, turning off his lights in the process. Without hesitation, he ran back toward the shed and hid around the thorny hedge that surrounded the property. He could still see Celeste inside the house, but she was now up from her chair and slowly moving toward the center of the front room. She approached the front door and looked around to make sure nobody was watching. She made her way down the sidewalk and into the trees on the other side of the dirt lot next to the shed. Suddenly, Edward spotted a set of headlights turn on, as he quickly made his way back to where he had parked his car. Hiding behind the front of the car and hidden by the darkened foliage, Edward watched as Celeste drove down the unlit street. He carefully got back in his car and waited until her black sedan made its way around the corner. Within seconds, he was directly behind her, not more than 30 yards from the back of her car. Edward could feel his heart practically beat through his chest, while he tried to gather his thoughts. Where was Celeste going? Hopefully, she would take him to the answers that would somehow save a life that had truly gone mad.

Abby staggered to her chair and felt the impact of Benjamin's words literally take her breath away. Oh my gosh, Abby thought, Benjamin's mother was dead before Conners hit her! Abby made her way over to the sink and threw cold water on her face, hoping the bad dream would somehow go away. What in the world was she going to do now? The case had just been decided and now she was sitting on the information that could, in fact, set Edward Conners free. She made her way back over to Benjamin and held him just as tight as she could, hoping to find a way to garner some of his pain. Benjamin finally let Abby go, but not before telling her what was on his mind. "Miss Abby, I have a question for you," said Benjamin, as his intuitive side was about to kick into overdrive. "Do you have any kids at home like me? You sure do have a way with kids, Miss Abby, and what you say always seems to make a lot of sense." Abby took a deep breath and stared back into Benjamin's blue eyes. She was falling in love with this little boy, and she quickly tried to regain her thoughts and answer his heartfelt question. "Benjamin, I don't have any children of my own, but I've always loved kids," responded Abby, while she felt a smile embrace her tired face. "You are such a sweet boy, and I'd do anything in the world for you." Benjamin looked up at Abby and felt a smile take hold of his face as well. Without any hesitation, his question back to Abby was an easy one, "Miss Abby, would you please be my mommy?" Abby put her arms around Benjamin and started to cry. He felt her heart melt against his, and for a very brief moment in time, Benjamin could almost feel the presence of his mother right there with him as well. "Oh, Benjamin," answered Abby. "We will see, sweetheart. We will see."

Chapter Twelve

The Committee

C eleste pulled up at the end of the street and turned around to make sure she was alone. Coast is clear, she thought, as she began to make her way up toward the familiar cottage at the end of the cobblestone walk. Close behind, adjacent to the path she was on, stood Edward as he watched intently to see where Celeste was going. He moved as close as possible without being seen and slowly looked through the portable binoculars that were hanging from his neck. Celeste made her way up to the front door and entered the code 47381, and the door opened. Nobody was there to greet her, but she knew from memory where she was expected to be. As always, the house was dark except for the dim light that waited for her on the other side of the old, brown curtain. Quickly, Edward ran as fast as he could to the door and entered the code as well. The door opened and to Edward's surprise, nobody was there to meet him. Quickly, he made his way to the closet door on his left and entered the pitch black space. He could literally feel the shirt on his chest rise up and down with the beating of his heart, while his adrenaline was now running at full tilt. Somehow, he had to get himself together, or he would never survive the night. Edward reached into his vest and took out the tiny microphone that led to the recorder in his side pocket. Click…the recorder was now on. Hopefully, it would capture the activity on the other side of the curtain. Edward took a deep breath and wiped the sweat from his brow. He had no idea who was in the other room, but he had a very strong suspicion that the discussion would eventually focus on him. Edward would not be disappointed, but was he ready for what was about to come his way?

"Benjamin, will you wait here for just a minute?" asked Abby, as she knew she had to move quickly. "I need to run out into the hallway but I'll be right back, ok? I promise I'll be right back." "I understand, Miss Abby," replied Benjamin. "I trust you. I know you won't leave me." Abby made her way out into the hallway and ran straight to the office of her good friend, Terrance Wilson. "Terrance, I'm so sorry for barging in here like this, but I really need to speak with you about something. Do you have a quick minute?" Terrance looked up from the piles of paperwork sitting on the corner of his desk and replied, "What is it, Abby? As you can see, I have a ton of work to do, but I know you wouldn't be here if it wasn't important. Now, what's on your mind?" Abby took a deep breath and felt her voice begin to quiver. Terrance could see that something was wrong and jumped right in to help her along. "Abby, slow down just a minute and have a seat," said Terrance, as he pulled the chair out away from the wall. "Just take your time and wait until you catch your breath." Abby nodded her head in agreement and sat down next to her trusted friend. "Terrance, there's a boy here named Benjamin Sanders. I'm sure you've heard all about him." Terrance interrupted Abby and responded, "I know all about him, Abby. He's a special, little boy who's been through a lot. In fact, I've instructed my staff to keep a close eye on him during the trial. We didn't want to place him into a foster care home until things settled down a bit. Now that the trial has ended, we're hoping the media moves on to something else and their infatuation with Benjamin simmers. Up until now, we've done our best to protect him. I think we've done a good job of isolating him from the questions that will only bring him back to the loss of his mother. The little guy needs to move on with his life, which is going to be very difficult." Abby nodded her head in agreement and replied, "That's why I'm here, Terrance. Benjamin and I have really connected over the past couple of weeks. When I was younger, I lost my mother and sister in a car crash that devastated me and my world. Thank God, I still had my dad, and he helped me get through the painful nights. Benjamin doesn't have a mother or father now, and I can't even imagine what he's going through. I do know that my loss at an early age raised a lot of questions for me regarding my faith and why God allowed the accident to happen. Through a lot of prayer, I was able to move on and put my total trust in Him, even though there were still a lot of unanswered questions. I came to the realization that these questions will always be there for me, and that He will explain everything to me when I see Him in heaven. I know in my heart that Benjamin has the same questions right now, Terrance. I can help him. I'd like to start the process of adopting little Benjamin. Right now, my immediate family in Cradle Ridge consists of Chester, my golden lab. I know he'd love to have Benjamin join us because he needs someone to play with every day. It goes without saying, Terrance, that my dad would love to have a grandson as well. Simply put...I need him just as much as he needs me."

Edward rested his shoulder on the inside of the closet wall, while he waited for the voices to appear in the other room. Waiting to see who Celeste was meeting with was difficult for Edward, as the silence seemed to suffocate his every thought. What if he was found in the closet? There was no doubt in his mind that if he was found, he would be dead. Although he had been a man of zero faith in his life, Edward found himself beginning to pray for the very first time. Funny how the realization of imminent death will do that to a guy, he thought, as he began to mouth the words silently under his breath. "I have no idea what to say to you, God, but if you're out there, please protect me," begged Edward, as he closed his eyes. "Please, find a way to somehow keep me safe." Edward could hear the shuffling of feet in the other room, and then everything came to a stop. It was time for the meeting to begin...

"Celeste, we're gathered here this evening because of the serious nature of your final report back to the committee," stated Mize, as he peered into the eyes of Celeste from the head of the darkened table. Celeste looked around the room and could tell from the faces directed her way that anything less than a glowing report would be unacceptable to the committee. She took a deep breath and began to deliver the feedback they had been waiting for...hopefully; it would be met with their approval. "Mr. Mize, I met with Conners tonight. As I indicated before, he bought into this entire charade the first night in his cell, and I'm happy to report that nothing was different tonight. From the first time I met him, he's been a desperate man searching for the infamous mother lode." Celeste wasn't about to inform Mize that Edward showed uncommon hesitation earlier that evening, finally deciding on a third wish after her encouragement. This would only raise questions from Mize, and Celeste simply could not afford to take this risk...so she continued. "Conners's third wish is to get off on a misdemeanor with possible probation when the sentencing takes place next month. Based on our discussion and his naïve belief that this third wish will come true just like his first two, I do believe that he'll keep his mouth shut until sentencing is handed down." Mize interrupted Celeste, and she immediately backed down like a whimpering puppy. "Celeste, let me make this very clear to you. If he speaks up before the sentencing and causes a stir of any kind, it will cost you your life. So...let me ask you a simple question," stated Mize, as he moved closer to where Celeste was seated. "Is Conners going to stay quiet between now and sentencing, or do I need to get rid of him before it takes place?"

Edward could feel his heart drop to the floor, while he listened to the discussion regarding his fragile life. "Mr. Mize, Conners believes his third wish will come true because it's all he has to hold on to right now," responded Celeste. "He was a man without any hope when I came into his cell last year with this three wish proposal. He put his trust in me, and that was his first mistake. His state of mind was a mess, and he played right into our trap, just like we knew he would. I'm happy to say that I believe his mind is still a mess, and he'll hang on to this third wish until sentencing takes place. Obviously, there's no possible way the sentence handed out next month will be a misdemeanor. I believe he'll be booked on a felony charge, carrying with it at least 15 years in the state penitentiary. We all know that once the sentence is finalized and communicated, he'll be up the river without a paddle. His word will mean nothing." "Precisely, Celeste, and that's why we need to play this thing out right up until the sentence is communicated. I want to go back and quickly review the events leading up until tonight with this committee, answer any questions, and then adjourn with no further discussion on this topic until after the sentencing. Do I make myself clear?" "Yes, sir," answered the committee, in unison. "Good...if you have any questions when I'm going through this summary, you better jump in now or forever hold your peace. I don't want any surprises down the road."

"Abby, are you sure about this?" asked Terrance, as he sat back in his chair. "Benjamin has been through more than you and I will ever know, and he's going to need a lot of attention right now. Are you sure you're going to be able to give him what he needs, with your schedule and hectic pace of life?" "I need to find the time, Terrance," replied Abby. "My life has turned into nothing but work, and I believe this little guy has come into my world to show me what's truly important. You have my word. I will give him everything he needs, and I will commit my life to him." Terrance looked over at Abby and could tell by the tears in her eyes that she really did need Benjamin right now. Terrance reached over and grabbed the phone. "Hey, Bill, this is Terrance. Could you do me a favor? Let's stop everything regarding the transfer of Benjamin Sanders over to the foster home in Hidden Valley. I know they were looking at possibly bringing him in after the trial had ended, but I think we have another option that's a much better fit. I'll stop down in a few minutes and give you all the details. I think little Benjamin is going to be real happy when he finds out about his new home. Talk with you in a few minutes, Bill." Terrance hung up the phone and looked over at Abby. His smile told her everything she needed to know. Abby wrapped her arms around him and screamed just as loud as she could. She couldn't wait to go tell Benjamin...

Listening from just inside the closet door, Edward could hardly contain himself. How in the world would he ever maintain his composure, he thought, as the plan that shattered his life was about to be revealed on the other side of the door? He could feel his blood pulsate through his body, as his chest began to pound in anticipation of what was yet to come. Mize got up and began to make his way around the table, no more than 20 feet from where Edward was hiding. He knew a move of any kind on his part would undoubtedly cost him his life. Edward pressed his fist to his mouth and slowly bit down on his knuckled hand, as this seemed to help him focus on remaining calm and still. Mize looked around the table at each member of the committee. They were almost home, and their perfect plan was just about complete. The last thing Mize would tolerate at this juncture was a hiccup of any kind. Everything had to remain perfect.

"As we look back at the events of this past year, the reason we're here today is because we've been able to keep the identity of this committee in strict confidence," stated Mize, as he captured the attention of his targeted audience from the very first word. "Moving forward, nobody outside this room can ever find out about this committee or any of the events over this past year. Each of you was chosen because I trust you. If that trust is broken in any way, I will track you down and your disloyalty will cost you your life." Tension filled the room and seemed to suffocate every member of the committee. Nobody at the table said a word…except, of course, Mize. Edward could feel the adrenaline penetrate his entire body, while he braced himself for the information that was about to come his way. There was no way he could have ever prepared himself for what was about to spill out. "Now, let's go back to the beginning of this process. As I finish with each of you here tonight during this summary, I will be giving you a small briefcase. Inside the briefcase, you will find $1M in unmarked bills. This amount reflects your share of the $10M that was so kindly donated to this committee by our good friend, Mr. Edward Conners. In due time, he will realize that there really is no company with a magic microchip. I'm very proud to say that his $10M investment, by way of our old friend, Andrew Ridgeley III, is now in very good hands." And with that, laughter broke out around the table with Mize leading the way. With careful deliberation, he began to go around the table, methodically reviewing the sequence of events from start to finish. Turning to his right, he began with Clark Davis, Ridgeley's trusted advisor. "Clark, when you had Andrew sign the addendum regarding his estate, the verbiage in the addendum allowed for total transfer over to Edward Conners, correct?" Davis leaned forward in his chair and responded, "That's correct, Warren. I had the fine print in the addendum reflect transfer flexibility, which allowed me to move the entire $10M estate over to Conners. We simply altered the final agreement to fit into the first dream Conners communicated to Celeste, which gave us instant credibility with him moving forward. We sucked him into our trap on his first wish, and he was never able to recover. Quite frankly, Ridgeley never paid any attention to anything he ever signed, so this was easy. Sylvia's performance was so convincing when she found out she wasn't the beneficiary that word spread quickly throughout their circle of friends that she received nothing. Obviously, this was exactly what we needed to jumpstart the plan. Sylvia, you really should get an award for that performance!" Sylvia reached out across the table, playfully grabbed Davis's hand,

and replied, "Oh, Clark, you're just way too nice. This was easy for me because I've absolutely despised Conners for years. He sponged off my husband for a long time, so this entire operation has been very personal for me. I knew the money would end up back in our hands eventually. Clark, you were amazing as well." Edward felt frozen in the closet, while the story continued to evolve on the other side of the curtain. Somehow, he had to find a way to separate himself from the words that were ripping him apart piece by piece... and they were just getting started.

Mize moved closer to Sylvia and reached down and gave her a kiss on the neck, "You were incredible, sweetheart," said Mize. "We're almost home. Let me ask you a couple of quick questions just to make sure we aren't forgetting anything. When you gave Andrew the sedative that eventually knocked him out on the drive that morning, you did make sure you got rid of everything, correct?" Sylvia stood up and moved closer to Mize, and responded, "Honey, I told you. I knew Andrew was heading out on a drive that morning because he was very upset about the start of the market and what was happening. I put the three pills in his juice just like you told me to do, right after I confirmed that he would soon be leaving the house. Based on what you told me, I knew the pills would knock him out in approximately 12 minutes. In light of the fact that he had 20 minutes of sharp corners just above the ravine, I knew there was no way he would make it with the three pills already on board. Just like we planned, he hit the tree at about the 13-minute mark and died instantly. This opened the door for the eventual transfer of the estate over to Conners, which we had to do in order to make sure nobody was on to us." Mize just smiled, while he looked Sylvia's way, "This is why I love you so much, baby, and why you and I are going to be together very soon. You are so bad!"

Mize moved around the side of the table and began to review the next series of events as well. He had to make sure nothing was taken for granted. "Ok, so now Conners is thrown into the middle of this due to the estate transfer, and we had to find a way to get rid of him. Luckily for us, he did all the dirty work so we didn't have to. We put a tail on him later that night because we figured the shock of Ridgeley's death would cause him to do something stupid. We didn't want to get rid of him because it would complicate things, but we knew it was just a matter of time before the combination of Ridgeley's departure and his financial mess collided. Sylvia's two phone calls to Conners pushed the poor sap over the edge, and the rest is history. Initially, we thought about finding a way to pin the case on him, but instead, we decided to wait and watch his every move. He was the perfect target. When Conners hit the parked car with that woman inside, he opened the door for me to become his lawyer. He had no idea what he had signed up for, and I knew it was just a matter of time before he fell into our web of deception. I quickly locked that jury in from the very start, subsequently gained Conners's trust, and then I intentionally slip up and hand Conners over to the hungry wolves during our closing argument. Am I brilliant or what?" Mize looked out at his team for confirmation, knowing full well that he was in absolute control of the committee's every move. As each of the members anxiously awaited payment, nobody was in a position to argue, and everyone nodded in agreement. "So, we've heard from Davis, Sylvia, and Celeste. Here are your respective payouts, as per our agreement. Jenkins, you pulled the necessary strings to get Celeste into Conners's prison cell for his first wish, which was perfect. After his first wish was shared with Celeste, you took him directly to Thomas's limo the next morning. Guys, was there anything during the transfer that needs to be discussed?" Thomas shook his head "no" and simply replied, "Not a thing, boss. The next phase of the plan went just as we planned. Conners responded the way we thought he would." Officer Jenkins replied as well, "Warren, we had to get him out on bail. I released him and made sure there was no trail back to you. No reference regarding the money you posted, and Conners was out in a flash. We handed him over to you, and the game was on." "Good work, guys," responded Mize. "Here's your payment as well. Looks like we're down to you, Fletcher, our final member of the team. I must compliment you. You moved that jury our way. Excellent work, here you go." Fletcher looked over at Mize and cracked a smile. "My pleasure, boss," replied Fletcher, as he set the briefcase on the floor between his legs. Mize looked over at the committee members and made one last remark. He had to be very clear with his closing statement...there would be no gray area in his delivery. "Committee members, we are at the final stage of this operation. Each of you is walking away from here tonight with $1M in unmarked bills. When we leave here at the conclusion of this meeting, we will not be speaking with anyone in this room ever again. Maybe we'll find a way to work together in the future, but it's going to be a very long time before that happens. Any communication, assuming it does take place one day, can only be initiated by me. All of us will need to lay low for awhile until the dust settles, and then we'll see what happens. Sylvia and I are going to be moving from the area as soon as Conners is in prison, but up until then, even we're not going to be seen together. The last piece of this beautiful puzzle is the sentencing, which will be taking place very soon. Conners is under the belief that his final wish with Celeste will guarantee him a misdemeanor charge and that he'll walk. He believes his $10M investment will allow him to subsequently run a company that is nothing but smoke and mirrors. When the sentencing is communicated, he'll realize that this entire three wish proposal was solely designed to utilize him as our tool to the $10M prize. We banked on one assumption, and that was his greed. Conners certainly didn't let us down. At the end of the day, he has nobody to blame but himself. Without his cooperation, this simply could not have been possible. Now, we must leave here separately and get back to our daily routine...without any disruptions whatsoever. Are there any questions?"

Edward could feel his heart begin to race, as he quickly made his way out of the closet and toward the front door.

Somehow, he had to get through that door without making a noise, or he would be dead. Edward carefully opened the front door and could hear the shuffling of feet behind him. Just as the door closed behind him, Sylvia entered the hallway right next to the closet where Edward had been standing. Never had the darkness looked so good, and Edward quickly made it to the side of the cottage. Without hesitation, he ran just as fast as he could to the end of the street. He could only hope that he hadn't been seen...

Abby made her way back into the room where Benjamin had been resting. Benjamin's eyes were closed, and Abby moved closer to the side of his bed. Abby stared at his little face and couldn't wait to give him the good news. How would he react, Abby thought, as she waited anxiously for his little blues to open. She sat next to his bed and couldn't help but think about all the things he had gone through when his world came crashing down. Oh, how she wanted to help him get on with his life and somehow get that awful night out of his mind. Abby knew firsthand the pain that Benjamin was feeling, but she also believed in her heart that God had brought her into his life for a reason. Slowly, Benjamin's eyes began to open, and there was his new best friend waiting for him. "Hi, Miss Abby," said Benjamin, as he began to sit up in his bed. "What are you doing here with me?" Abby took a deep breath and, for the first time in a very long while, she felt nervous at the thought of what she was about to say. "Benjamin, I have a very important question to ask you. You've been through a lot, and I know you miss your mommy very much. I know just how you're feeling because I miss my mommy too. There's not a day that goes by that I don't think of her. I can still smell her perfume at times, and then I remember our days together all over again. Benjamin, you're going to be leaving this place soon, and I know it's going to be very difficult for you. I've spoken to the person who's in charge here, and I told him I'd like to take you home with me. I would never try to replace your mommy, but I promise I'll love you and take care of you. If you don't want to come with me, I will understand. I would love to have you come home with me, and I know my dog, Chester, would love to have you too. Would you like to be part of our family, Benjamin?" Benjamin started to cry and reached up and put his arms around Abby. Finally, after all his tears had dampened Abby's left shoulder, Benjamin slowly pulled away and gathered up enough strength to answer her question. "Miss Abby," replied Benjamin. "I would love to come home with you. I promise I'll be a real good boy, and I'll take care of Chester if you want me to. I'm really going to miss my mommy a lot, but I know you'll be there for me. I'm going to be there for you if you need me too. I love you, Miss Abby. I'd love to come home with you and be a part of your family." Abby held on to Benjamin with everything she had and could feel the little boy's chest beat rapidly. Deep down inside, Abby knew exactly how Benjamin was feeling because she felt the same way when her mother died. On this particular day, the two of them had undoubtedly become one, and Abby could feel God's presence surround them.

Through His grace, they had somehow found each other. His timing was perfect once again...

Gasping for air, Edward made it into his house and shut the door behind him, while he fell to the floor in the darkened hallway. No matter how hard he tried, he just couldn't shake the discussion that just took place. Mize and his committee had completely ruined Edward's life, and all he could do now was wait for the final sentencing that could put him away for good. Edward reached into his pocket and removed the tape that had recorded the chain of events and their respective cast of characters. He lay on the cold, wooden floor and began to think back on everything that had taken place. Edward's mind began to race, while he found his anger quickly being replaced by the introspective shame and humiliation that had brought him to this point. As much as he despised Mize and his entourage, there was one thought that he couldn't shake free. Deep down inside, he knew he wouldn't be in this position today if it wasn't for his greed. This was, without question, the underlying cause for the successful implementation of the events that had brought him to this point in his life. Edward curled up on the floor and began to sob, as his whimpering cries echoed in the hallway that seemed to suffocate his every thought. Hopelessness was seeping into the crevice of his mind, and for the first time in his life, Edward's thoughts were focused on his own humility and personal surrender. He had never felt this way before and had, without a doubt, reached the lowest point in his life. He had reluctantly found the valley that wanted to consume him, as his fragile life was now spilled open for the world to see. Edward's mind began to take him back one more time, and then it hit him! For the first time in his life, he had actually prayed for God's help while standing in the closet outside the committee's final meeting. How in the world did he ever survive in a closet no more than 20 feet from the group that had literally taken his life away? There was no earthly explanation, Edward thought, that could support such a divine intervention. This was the first time in his life that he had prayed and he knew, without any question whatsoever, that God had protected him from the hands that would have wanted him dead. As Edward stared at the ceiling above, it was as if he could feel a softening of the heart that had become frozen over time. Instead of feeling bitter for what had taken place, Edward's thoughts were focused on how he could somehow make amends for what he had done. Edward knew the primary reason he was in the position he was in was due to the greed that had consumed his heart years ago. Rather than placing the blame on Mize and his committee, Edward wanted more of the God he turned to while he was in the closet. He took out the tape, closed his eyes, and knew in his heart what he needed to do. Edward went into his office and took out the yellow envelope, filled out the address, and threw the tape inside. Finally, he was ready to do what needed to be done…

Chapter Thirteen

Rising Above

Two weeks had transpired since Edward's visit to the cottage, and here he was now, the night before the sentencing that would impact his life forever. Slowly, Edward made his way to the floor next to his bed, and he knelt down and began to pray. His prayer tonight was very simple, one that had been on his heart for a very long time. "God, I ask that you have mercy on me and, please, forgive me," pleaded Edward, as he bowed his head. "In the past, I have been obsessed with money, never having quite enough to do the things that I wanted to do. Greed took over my mind, body, and soul… and I never had any time for you. I promise that from this point forward, I will do everything in my life for you. If I have to go to prison for the rest of my life, I am willing to do so. After the accident, I was given three wishes to save my life, and I put my trust and faith in the world and not in you. Tonight, I hope and pray that you will grant me one wish because nothing else in my life matters right now. My wish and my prayer tonight are one in the same…that I may live the rest of my life for you and have eternal salvation. I give my life to you, Lord, and I promise to always serve you in all that I do. Thank you for saving my life and for giving me a new heart. I promise to cherish it forever. Over this past year, my life was revealed for all to see. My greed and self-centered focus took me into a very dark world, but you reached down and pulled me out. I have no idea what will happen at the sentencing tomorrow, but I have peace with the outcome regardless of what it may be. I am grateful to be on your team now, and I promise to always keep my eyes on you...focused on what you want me to do, rather than what I want to do. Thank you for giving me a second chance at life. I will honor you in all that I do. I will not let you down." Edward wiped his tears away and pulled himself up on to his bed. On one of the most difficult nights of his life, peace had taken up residency in his heart and it felt real good. No matter what the outcome turned out to be, Edward knew his soul had been saved...and he would never be the same again.

All eyes were on Edward, while he made his way into the courtroom. Standing next to his client, Mize was all smiles. Leaning over toward Edward, Mize said, "You look different today, Edward. You're usually all bent out of shape. Today, you look relaxed. Are you feeling all right?" "Warren, I've never felt better than I do today," replied Edward. "It's great to see you again. You've been a stranger lately. No matter what happens today, Warren, I've already come out of this thing a winner." Mize looked over at Edward and felt an uneasiness come over him in a flash. What was it with

Conners today, Mize thought, as he continued to stare over at the stranger standing next to him? Mize began to think back on the events that had transpired since the last time he and Edward were together, but he just couldn't put his finger on the reason why his client seemed so different today. The more Edward smiled, the more uneasy Mize became...

"All rise, the court is now in session," said the bailiff, as the crowd stood in anticipation of the sentencing that was about to take place. "The honorable Judge Branson now presiding." Everything fell quiet, while Branson made his way to the front of the courtroom. His rules were about to be communicated, and there would be no room for any misinterpretation. "Ladies and gentlemen of this jury, I want to say thank you once again for your hard work since the beginning of this trial. I think you did a very good job with this case, considering the evidence that was presented. Mr. Edward Conners was found guilty of vehicular manslaughter, and all of us are here today to bring this case to closure. I am prepared to issue a sentence for Mr. Conners, but before I do, is there anyone on either of the legal teams with any questions or input regarding the process? Mr. Mize, do you have any questions?" Mize looked up at Judge Branson and replied, "No, your honor. I believe this entire process followed the law of the land to the tee. You did an exceptional job of keeping everything on target as well." "Thank you, Mr. Mize. Ms. Holt, how about you? Do you have any questions?" Abby took a deep breath and carefully thought about what to do next. Her next move would either be the safe move...or the right move. It had to be one or the other, but it couldn't be both. Abby reached down into her briefcase and took out the tape. Mize stared over from his chair on the other side of the room and watched his adversary begin to address the judge. Mize knew she was now entering uncharted waters, and this could mean disbarment for her if things went his way. What did she have in her hand, Mize thought, as he watched Abby begin to move closer toward Judge Branson. Edward watched from a distance, as he recognized the familiar tape make its way into the view of everyone on site. He could feel his pulse begin to race because he knew what that tape meant. Nobody in the courtroom would ever forget this day...

"Judge Branson, I need to meet with you in private before your sentence is read," said Abby, as the courtroom fell silent and watched her every move. "There's something you need to know." "Ms. Holt. You're asking me to do something that has never been done in my courtroom before. I'm getting ready to sentence your client, and you're asking me to meet with you in private. I've never done anything like this before in all my years on the bench. You are making a spectacle of my courtroom, and I don't like it one bit." Abby could feel the intense pressure from Branson almost reach out and slap her in the face, but she knew she had to push forward... even if it cost her everything. "Judge Branson, I understand and I would never ask this of you unless I knew that lives were literally hanging in the balance here today. I'd like to share something with you in your chambers, and if you don't think it's worthy of this interruption, then I will hand in my license here today. I will never practice law in this county ever again." Judge Branson turned to the side, removed his glasses, and gently put them inside his shirt pocket. "You have a deal, Ms. Holt. Now, follow me. Oh, and Mize, you may as well come in here too. Five minutes...that's all you have, Ms. Holt."

Mize followed Abby and Judge Branson into his chambers and slammed the door behind him, as he made his way toward the front of the room. Mize was furious and couldn't wait to rip into his younger counterpart. "Ms. Holt, this is a disgrace! I've been in more courtrooms than you'll ever set foot in, and I've never seen anything like this. You're making a fool out of Judge Branson here, and I'm going to push for your disbarment as soon as this escapade is over. For you to think that you can just waltz right into this courtroom at the 23rd hour and change the rules of the game is an insult to this entire profession." Abby had heard enough... she wasn't about to take this kind of treatment anymore. Today, Mize didn't scare her one bit! "You hold on right there, Mize. I think you better sit down and keep quiet. For you to be patronizing me by insinuating that I'm an insult to this profession is a joke. Have a seat, Mr. Mize. What you're about to hear will show everyone who the real disgrace is!" Before Judge Branson could intercede, Abby hit the "play" button and Mize's voice was as clear as day. Judge Branson leaned back in his chair, while Mize's voice on the recorder immediately brought him back to the meeting with his committee a short while ago. As Mize clearly described the plot involving Ridgeley's death and his scheme to steal the $10M, Branson began to shake his head in disgust. Abby simply looked over at Mize and continued to listen to the recording, while every word clearly dug even a deeper hole for Mize. "Mr. Mize, you orchestrated the death of Ridgeley and then you used your client to take the fall," stated Abby, as her newfound confidence took hold. "As evidenced by your own admission on this tape, you were the mastermind behind this plan from the very beginning. In addition to your damaging confession on tape, a very close source of mine has verified to me that Olivia Sanders was actually dead before your client's car hit her. Mize, your little game is over. You were willing to use everyone to get what you wanted, and in the end, you're the one who will finally get what you deserve."

Mize's piercing eyes began to turn a fiery red, and his hands started to tremble. Judge Branson could see from his vantage point that Mize was going to erupt and slowly began to move closer to where he was sitting. Suddenly, Mize jumped across the table and wrapped his hands around Abby's throat. Branson moved as quickly as he could to cut off Mize, but there was no way he could get there in time. Mize threw Abby to the ground and pounced on top of her like a wounded lion. Oh, how he wanted to end her life and stop this nonsense. In less than five minutes, Mize's entire plan unraveled...and all because of her! He dug his fingers into her throat and could hear the soft gurgling of her life slowly beginning to depart. Just one more squeeze, he thought, as he pushed with all his might. Judge Branson made his way over to Mize and knew he had to do something fast, or Abby would be dead. Rearing back with everything he had, Branson buried his size 12 into Mize's side and made direct contact with his exposed rib cage. Mize immediately fell to the floor and grabbed his side in excruciating pain, as he unwillingly let up on the squeezing of Abby's throat. Branson made his way over to the door and screamed for help. Within seconds, three guards were inside and had Mize pinned against the floor. Branson leaned over Abby to see if she was still alive and whispered, "It's ok, Ms. Holt. Mize is not going to hurt you anymore. We're going to get you to the hospital and you're going to be all right. Don't try to talk right now. We have help on its way. Just hang in there. Please, hang in there."

Chaos engulfed the courtroom, as everyone pushed their way toward the judge's chambers to see where the screaming and yelling originated. At the front of pack was Edward, as he made his way inside before the door slammed behind him. On the floor in front of him was Abby, face scratched and neck bloodied due to the force of Mize's uncontrollable tirade. Edward felt his heart drop to the floor, as he moved closer to the woman he barely knew. Guilt immediately came over him because he realized he had put her in harm's way with the tape that indicted Mize and his committee. Edward weaved his way through the debris and made his way to where Abby was lying. "Ms. Holt, I am so sorry about this. Please, stay with me, Ms. Holt. God has His hands around you right now. I can feel it." Abby's eyes slowly opened and she felt God's presence immediately enter the room. Mouthing the words softly, Abby reached out and touched Edward's hand. "Thank you, Mr. Conners. This is not your fault." And with that, Abby closed her eyes and fell asleep.

Mize felt his face slam against the walls of Branson's chambers. Branson yelled out to the guards who had him pinned, "Take that man down to the holding pen right now. Charge him with assault and contempt of court to begin with. Those charges are just the beginning for Mr. Mize!" Screaming as they pulled him across the floor, Mize lashed out at Edward, who was just on the other side of the rubble in the center of the room. "Conners, I'm going to make you pay for what you've done. You will never be safe! I own this town, Conners, and you will never get away." Edward watched intently, as Mize disappeared into the corridor. Quickly, his attention moved back over to Abby, who was being placed on the stretcher. The paramedics surrounded her and moved as quickly as they could through the cameras waiting on the other side of the door. Pictures were snapped of the war zone inside Branson's chambers, while Edward watched from a distance. Moving over to the corner of the room, Edward found much-needed solace and began to focus his prayers on Abby. His temporary satisfaction regarding Mize's sudden implosion was far outweighed by his real concern for her right now. . .

"Mr. Holt, this is the Cradle Ridge Medical Center," said the lead nurse, Lynn Able, as she quickly moved into the reason for her call. "Your daughter has been injured and was admitted into the hospital about 30 minutes ago. It says here that you live in Idaho, so I don't want you to think that you have to get on the first plane out of town to see her. In fact, we've stabilized her now and it looks like she's going to be ok. We just wanted you to be aware that she's in the hospital and will more than likely be here for awhile. I wish I had more information for you, but I don't at this time. I will call you as soon as I have an update." William tried to catch his breath and get his bearings regarding his little girl's condition. "What happened, ma'am?" asked William, as he sat down in his chair next to the kitchen table. "What happened to my little girl?" Lynn could hear the concern in William's voice and immediately did all she could to put him at ease. "There was an altercation at the courthouse today, and I know your daughter got caught up in the middle of it. I'm sure there will be a lot more information on the local news here tonight because everyone is talking about it. I'm not sure if you'll hear about it or not in Idaho, but you just might. This whole case has been a real big thing around here. Your daughter has become kind of a celebrity with all the locals. She's going to be getting a lot of real good care here, Mr. Holt. Trust me when I tell you this, sir. Everybody here wants her to get better real soon." William hung up the phone and felt his mind going back to days gone by. Abby was all he had right now…she was his everything.

News quickly spread throughout the county that Mize was taken into custody, and warrants were issued for the arrest of his committee members as well. The sequence of events that had taken place had turned the community upside down, but for the first time in a very long while, the feeling among the locals was finally one of closure. Many in the area had always viewed Mize as being untouchable, so the idea of him being taken into custody created a jolt of newly-acquired confidence...one that hadn't been seen by the residents in a very long time. Judge Branson secured the tape and began the process of clearing Edward of all charges. Notification quickly made its way to Edward, and he knew without question that his prayers had been answered once again. In light of everything that had happened, there was something that he needed to do. There was one person that he just had to see...

Edward made his way through the entrance of the hospital and searched for the information desk that would hopefully lead him to where he needed to go. "Can I help you, sir?" asked the woman from behind the desk. "Yes, ma'am, I'm looking for Abby Holt," replied Edward. "Can you tell me what room she's in?" Looking down at the chart in front of her, the woman replied, "Room 331, sir. Just take the elevator over there to the third floor and then take a left. It's on the right side of the hallway about halfway down." Edward nodded his head and responded, "Thanks for your help, ma'am. I really appreciate it." He entered the elevator and before he knew it, he was fast approaching Abby's room. Edward could feel his pulse begin to race, as he moved closer to the door. Slowly, he opened the door and entered the room. Next to Abby's bed was Benjamin, which caught Edward totally off-guard. Edward felt frozen in his tracks, while he looked over at the little boy with the blue eyes. Before Edward had time to react, Benjamin turned his head and their eyes met. Edward waived and whispered, "Hi, Benjamin." Benjamin waived back toward Edward and gave him the most beautiful smile he had ever seen. Forgiveness had always been just a word for Edward, but thanks to Benjamin, the word would take on a whole different meaning from this day forward. He moved closer to where Abby was resting and sat down next to Benjamin. On his little lap was the Bible that Abby had given him. It was then that Edward knew, beyond any question, that God had brought him into Abby's room for a reason. As he looked down at her, Edward could feel a connection that was indescribable. Abby's eyes slowly began to open, with her smile not far behind. Looking up at Benjamin and Edward, Abby could sense that something was much different for her today. "I am so sorry, Abby," said Edward, as he looked down at her swollen face and neck. "I had no idea this was going to happen to you. I would have never sent you the tape had I known you were going to get hurt in the process."

Abby gathered up enough strength to reach out and touch Edward's hand. There was something she needed to say. "Edward, I don't blame you for this. Benjamin and I are together now and, for that, I am grateful. I will never be able to replace his mother, but in a divine way, I feel incredibly connected to her through her beautiful, little boy. God has covered us with His grace, and we will always have each other. You did nothing wrong. I don't hold you responsible for any of this...you simply did what you needed to do. Thank you so much for stopping by. It really means a lot to me that you are here." Benjamin looked up at Edward and put his arms out, hoping for a much-needed hug. Edward wrapped his arms around Benjamin and could feel the warmth of the little boy's heart grab on to him like a fire on a cold winter's night. It was on this day in the hospital room that Edward's life would be changed forever...this was, in fact, the day that he saw God's beauty shine through all the pain. Never in his life had Edward felt so much love in one room, and he knew that God had brought him the gift he needed the most. Finally, after many years of sadness and greed, Edward had been blessed with the family he had only dreamed about...the one that truly made him whole. The life he once knew was officially gone forever, and from this point forward, Edward would be focused on what truly mattered. Abby and Benjamin would become his everything, the indisputable reason for his existence. And although he could never replace the losses that both of them had faced, Edward knew that God had brought them together for a reason.

The years flew by at record pace, and the three of them would grow closer and closer to one another...and closer to God as well. For in the end, it was *Him*, and nobody else, who had truly made them one. Benjamin, the little boy with the big, blue eyes had somehow persevered through unthinkable pain. By the grace of God Himself, Benjamin had found the family he needed the most...and he would never be afraid again.

Chapter 14

Conclusion

Proverbs 19:21…
"Many are the plans in a man's heart, but it is the
Lord's purpose that prevails."

The world's barometer regarding success is one of the
most misunderstood concepts in our lives today. As
we continue to put our stock in things like the size of our
house, the kind of car we drive, and the circle of friends
we keep, many of the most important things in life fall by
the waist side. Faith and family have taken a back seat to
the possessions of this world, and in the process, a person's
life is here and gone before we know it. Similar to the life
of Edward Conners, many on earth will have to experience
their own personal fall from grace before their wake-up call
is answered. *The Visitor…Three Wishes for a Life* is an illus-
tration of just how powerful the temptation of personal greed
can be…how we as a society have placed value on material
possessions that have no relevant worth. My hope and prayer
is that this story creates a renewed sense of urgency for all

to embrace the joys that surround us each and every day, and that we resist the temptation of falling into the same trap that Edward Conners fell into. Remember...he was one of the few who made it out alive. Unfortunately, for most in the world today, their escape from self-destruction will be futile and their perpetual death will be imminent. However, as clearly illustrated in *The Visitor...Three Wishes for a Life,* it doesn't have to be this way. Just like Edward Conners, each one of us has a choice to make, the free will to go down the right path. And although the path is straight and narrow, there is room for all...and God is there to help us every step of the way.

CPSIA information can be obtained
at www.ICGtesting.com
Printed in the USA
FSOW02n0855181116
27556FS

9 781619 966260